Windows
one step at a time

BOOKS AVAILABLE

By both authors:

BP294 A Concise Introduction to Microsoft Works
BP306 A Concise Introduction to Ami Pro 3
BP319 Making MS-DOS work for you
BP327 DOS one step at a time
BP336 A Concise User's Guide to Lotus 1-2-3 Release 3.4
BP337 A Concise User's Guide to Lotus 1-2-3 for Windows
BP341 MS-DOS 6 explained
BP343 A concise introd'n to Microsoft Works for Windows
BP346 Programming in Visual Basic for Windows
BP351 WordPerfect 6 explained
BP352 Excel 5 explained
BP353 WordPerfect 6.0 for Windows explained
BP354 Word 6 for Windows explained
BP362 Access one step at a time
BP372 CA-SuperCalc for Windows explained
BP387 Windows one step at a time*
BP388 Why not personalise your PC
BP399 Windows 95 one step at a time*
BP400 Windows 95 explained
BP402 MS Office one step at a time
BP405 MS Works for Windows 95 explained
BP406 Word 95 explained
BP407 Excel 95 explained
BP409 MS Office 95 one step at a time
BP415 Using Netscape on the Internet*
BP419 Using Microsoft Explorer on the Internet*

By Noel Kantaris:

BP232 A Concise Introduction to MS-DOS
BP250 Programming in FORTRAN 77
BP258 Learning to Program in C
BP259 A Concise Introduction to UNIX*
BP261 A Concise Introduction to Lotus 1-2-3
BP264 A Concise Advanced User's Guide to MS-DOS
BP274 A Concise Introduction to SuperCalc 5
BP284 Programming in QuickBASIC
BP314 A Concise Introduction to Quattro Pro 3.0
BP325 A Concise User's Guide to Windows 3.1
BP330 A Concise User's Guide to Lotus 1-2-3 Release 2.4

Windows
one step at a time

by

N. Kantaris
and
P.R.M. Oliver

BERNARD BABANI (publishing) LTD.
THE GRAMPIANS
SHEPHERDS BUSH ROAD
LONDON W6 7NF
ENGLAND

PLEASE NOTE

Although every care has been taken with the production of this book to ensure that any projects, designs, modifications and/or programs, etc., contained herewith, operate in a correct and safe manner and also that any components specified are normally available in Great Britain, the Publishers and Author(s) do not accept responsibility in any way for the failure (including fault in design) of any project, design, modification or program to work correctly or to cause damage to any equipment that it may be connected to or used in conjunction with, or in respect of any other damage or injury that may be so caused, nor do the Publishers accept responsibility in any way for the failure to obtain specified components.

Notice is also given that if equipment that is still under warranty is modified in any way or used or connected with home-built equipment then that warranty may be void.

First Published – August 1995
Reprinted – December 1996

British Library Cataloguing in Publication Data

Kantaris, Noel
  Windows: One Step at a Time
  1. Title II. Oliver, Phil
  005.446

  ISBN 0 85934 387 1

Printed and Bound in Great Britain by Cox & Wyman Ltd, Reading

ABOUT THIS BOOK

Windows - One Step at a Time has been written for those who would like to know what to do next, when they are confronted with a screen full of Windows icons. It is a very basic book and is not intended as a complete guide to Windows. No previous knowledge of the Windows environment is assumed. For more comprehensive coverage of the Windows environment, including its accessories, we suggest you refer to the book *A Concise User's Guide to Windows 3.1* (BP325).

However, neither of these two books describes how to set up your computer hardware, or how to use the DOS operating system. If you need to know more about the latter topic, then we suggest that you select an appropriate level book for your needs from the 'Also Available' list - the books are graduated in complexity with the less demanding *One Step at a Time* series, followed by the *Concise Introduction* series, followed by the *Concise User's guide* series, to the more detailed *Explained* series. They are all published by BERNARD BABANI (publishing) Ltd.

This book can be used with Windows 3.0, Windows 3.1 and Windows for Workgroups 3.11, and is meant to simplify, supplement and, in some cases, to explain the documentation that came with your Windows package.

The first chapter gives an overview of the Windows environment and lays the foundations for later chapters, which cover, one step at a time, how to manipulate Windows, use the Control Panel to change your printer and optimise Windows to your system's hardware, use the Write and Notepad programs to read all those **Read Me** and **Update** files, use the ClipBoard/ClipBook facility to transfer information from one Windows application to another, use the File Manager to manage your work, create and manage Program Groups, install new application packages, and use the Print Manager to control your printing work.

This book was written with the busy person in mind. It is not necessary to learn all there is to know about a subject, when reading a few selected pages can usually do the same thing quite adequately!

With the help of this book, it is hoped that you will be able to come to terms with the Windows environment and get the most out of your computer in terms of efficiency, productivity and enjoyment, and that you will be able to do it in the shortest, most effective and informative way.

ABOUT THE AUTHORS

Noel Kantaris graduated in Electrical Engineering at Bristol University and after spending three years in the Electronics Industry in London, took up a Tutorship in Physics at the University of Queensland. Research interests in Ionospheric Physics, led to the degrees of M.E. in Electronics and Ph.D. in Physics. On return to the UK, he took up a Post-Doctoral Research Fellowship in Radio Physics at the University of Leicester, and then in 1973 a lecturing position in Engineering at the Camborne School of Mines, Cornwall, (part of Exeter University), where since 1978 he has also assumed the responsibility for the Computing Department.

Phil Oliver graduated in Mining Engineering at Camborne School of Mines in 1967 and since then has specialised in most aspects of surface mining technology, with a particular emphasis on computer related techniques. He has worked in Guyana, Canada, several Middle Eastern countries, South Africa and the United Kingdom, on such diverse projects as: the planning and management of bauxite, iron, gold and coal mines; rock excavation contracting in the UK; international mining equipment sales and international mine consulting for a major mining house in South Africa. In 1988 he took up a lecturing position at Camborne School of Mines (part of Exeter University) in Surface Mining and Management.

ACKNOWLEDGEMENTS

We would like to thank colleagues at the Camborne School of Mines for the helpful tips and suggestions which assisted us in the writing of this book.

TRADEMARKS

CONTENTS

1. PACKAGE OVERVIEW

Windows is a Graphical User Interface (GUI) program, which acts as a graphical front end to the Disc Operating System (DOS). Windows 3.11 (also known as Windows for Workgroups) is an upgrade to Windows 3.1, permitting faster access to your hard disc.

In general, Windows simplifies all the DOS operations by converting what you would normally have to type at the DOS prompt, into icons and pull-down menus. The basic package comes with its own 'Program', 'File', and 'Print' Managers, and a number of 'accessory' programs, including a word processor called 'Write', a graphics program called 'Paintbrush', a flat-file database called 'Cardfile', and a text editor called 'Notepad'. The three managers and some of the accessory programs, such as the Clipboard in the case of Windows 3.1 and the Clipbook in the case of Windows 3.11, will be discussed in some detail. Of course, Windows caters for many new technological developments, but the description of these is beyond the scope of this book.

One of the strengths of Windows lies in its ability to manage all other programs that run on your computer, whether these programs were specifically written for the Windows environment or not. Windows allows easy communication between such programs, but to what extent depends on the type of hardware at your disposal.

If the programs you want to use on your computer were specifically written to run under Windows, then you only need to master Windows to be able to manage these other programs quite well, as Windows applications are written to look and feel substantially the same as the Windows program which controls their environment. This means, of course, that you can save a large amount of time by cutting down on the learning curve of each new program you intend to use.

Hardware Requirements

If Windows is already installed on your computer, you can safely skip the rest of this chapter.

To install Windows 3.1, you need an IBM-compatible computer equipped with Intel's 80286, (or higher), processor, with a random access memory (RAM) requirement which is dependent on the type of processor (see below). Installing Windows for Workgroups (3.11) requires at least an 80386 processor with at least 4MB of RAM.

Installing Windows 3.1 on an 80286 machine requires 6.0MB of hard disc space (9MB is recommended), while installing it on an 80386 (or higher) processor machine, it requires 8MB (10MB is recommended). These two different modes of running Windows depend on the type of processor your computer is using, as well as the amount of available RAM in your computer. These are:

Standard mode   if you have an 80286 processor with 1MB or more of RAM, of which at least 256KB is extended memory,

Enhanced mode   if you have an 80386SX or higher processor with 2MB or more of RAM, of which at least 1MB is extended memory.

Installing Windows 3.11, requires 10.5MB of free disc space (15.5MB is recommended).

Realistically, to run todays Windows' software you need a 486 or a Pentium PC with preferably 8MB of RAM.

Although it is possible to operate Windows from the keyboard, the availability of a mouse is highly desirable. After all, pointing and clicking at an option on the screen to start an operation, or pointing and double-clicking at an icon to start a program, is a lot easier than having to learn several different key combinations.

Installing Windows

Installing Windows on your computer's hard disc is made very easy with the use of the SETUP program, which even configures Windows automatically to take advantage of the computer's hardware. You need to run the SETUP program because part of its job is to convert compressed Windows files from the distribution discs prior to copying them onto your hard disc.

However, before you start installing Windows, make sure you are not running any memory resident programs such as APPEND or GRAPHICS, to mention but two. If you have any entries in your **autoexec.bat** file that cause such programs to run, use the **Edit** screen editor and disable the relevant commands by adding the REM statement in front of them. Having done so, restart your computer by pressing the three key combination <Ctrl+Alt+Del> simultaneously.

To start installation, insert the Microsoft Windows distribution disc #1 into drive A:, log onto it by typing A: and pressing the <Enter> key, then type

   SETUP

at the A:\> prompt and press <Enter>. After a few seconds the first of several set-up screens is displayed in which the program offers you two alternative methods of installing itself; 'Express Setup', or 'Custom Setup' - the first for most users, and the second for experienced users only. From here on, follow the instructions on these screens.

The SETUP program detects your computer's processor and display, and if you have chosen the 'Express Setup' option, configures Windows to run with your system. If, on the other hand, you have chosen the 'Custom Setup', the program presents you with information and asks for verification about your system, such as type of computer, monitor, mouse, keyboard, and language used, but also gives you control over any changes to your **config.sys** and **autoexec.bat** files.

Installing a Printer:

When you choose to install a printer, SETUP presents you with a **List of Printers** from which you can choose the particular printer or printers you want to use, as shown below.

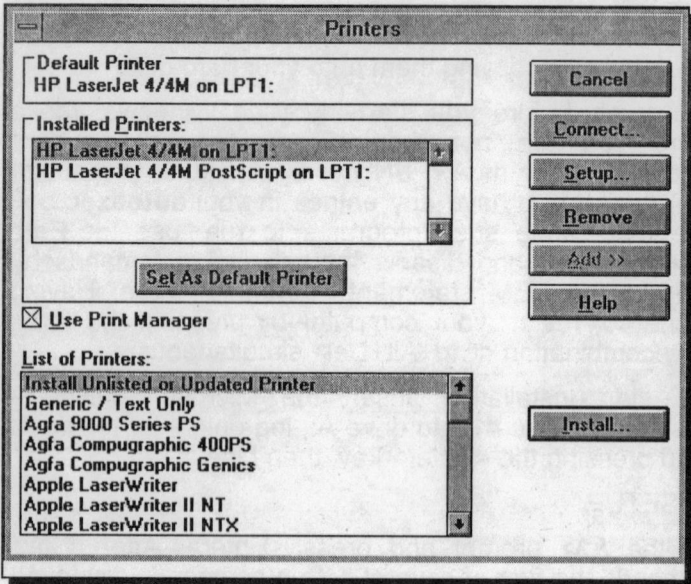

Here, two printer drivers were installed; an HP LaserJet 4/4M as the 'default' printer, and an HP LaserJet 4/4M PostScript printer, both configured for output via the parallel port LPT1. The choice of installing an additional printer driver could be dependent on whether such a printer was available to you at, say, your office on a shared basis. This would allow the preparation of documents incorporating fonts and styles, not available on the printer connected to your system, to be saved with your file and printed later on a printer which supports such enhancements.

4

Setting Up Applications:

The next step in the Windows SETUP is the search by the program of your computer's hard disc(s) to allow you to set up applications to run under Windows. Some of these applications might be standard DOS controlled applications, others might have been written specifically to run under Windows. Selecting the 'Search for applications' option and specifying the drive, displays a screen similar to the one below.

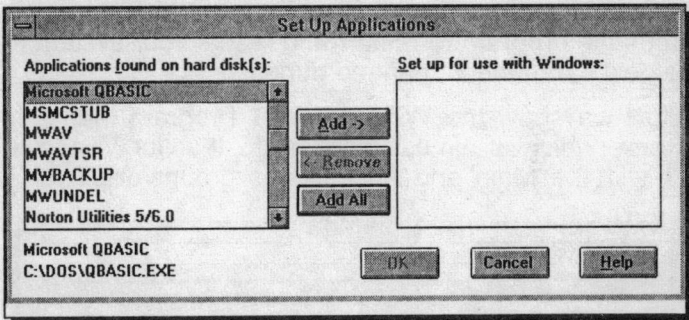

Adding applications to Windows can be done at a later stage - you might have to do this every time you add a new application you want to run in the Windows environment.

Next, use the mouse pointer to point and click at applications you would like to run under Windows. This highlights the application and at the same time produces an icon, to be used in conjunction with that application. You can look at more applications on the list by clicking at the down-arrow at the bottom of the scroll bar which appears to the right of the list of named applications.

Once you have highlighted all the applications you would like to add to Windows, press the **Add**⇒ button. The selected applications are then transferred to the right-hand side of the display. Pressing the **OK** button sets up these applications for use with Windows.

Completing Installation

If you are installing Windows with the 'Custom Setup' option, you will need to look into some final points to complete installation. For example, you need to specify the country, language and keyboard layout of your system, because SETUP doesn't always make the correct choice.

If, on the other hand, you are upgrading Windows, all that remains in order to exit SETUP is to select the **Restart Windows** option from the next display which forces the program to restart and resets your system to the new parameters changed during set up.

Below we show the Windows 3.11 Program Manager screen, which is almost identical to that for Windows 3.1, with the 'Main' and 'Accessories' groups displayed.

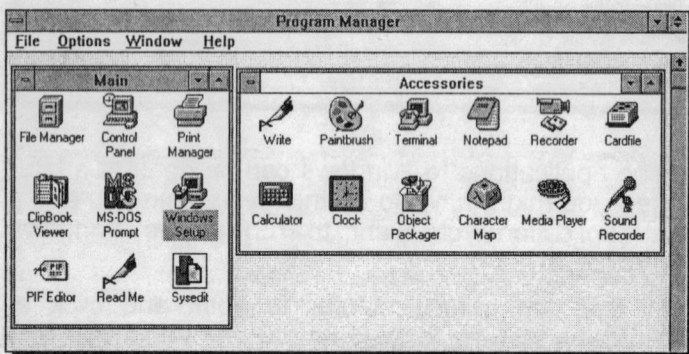

To change any of the hardware settings selected during installation, double click at the **Windows Setup** icon of the Main group of applications (shown selected in the above screen dump), then click **Options** on the menu bar and select the **Change System Settings** sub-menu from which you can change the 'Display', 'Keyboard', 'Mouse', and 'Network' options.

To change other hardware settings, you will have to use the 'Control Panel' as described later.

2. STARTING WINDOWS

To start Windows you need only type the word

    win

at the C:\> prompt. When the program is loaded, a screen similar to the following display appears on your screen. The differences depend primarily on whether you are using Windows 3.1, instead of Windows 3.11.

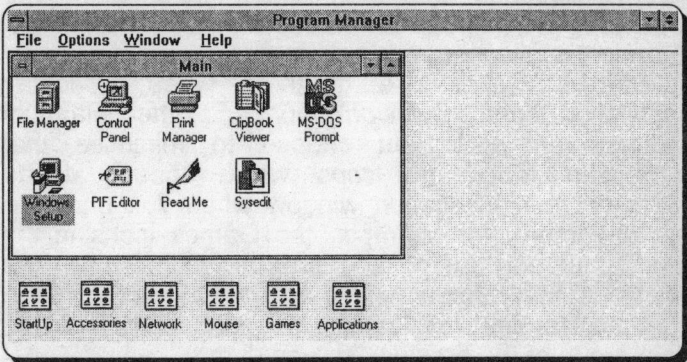

This easy way of starting up the program was arranged by SETUP when you allowed it to modify the contents of your system's **autoexec.bat** file, by the addition of the \WINDOWS directory into the PATH command. Indeed, it is imperative that the \WINDOWS directory is part of the PATH, otherwise Windows will not work. (Don't try to start the program with a batch file - it won't work properly). If you want Windows to be loaded automatically when you switch on your computer, then edit your **autoexec.bat** file and add the statement **win** at the very end of the file.

If you have any problems in loading Windows or running the program in a satisfactory manner, first refer to the documentation that comes with the package to make sure you have interpreted correctly the advice given, before you call Microsoft's customer service.

The Windows Screen

It is perhaps worth spending some time looking at the various parts that make up the Windows screen - we use the word 'Windows' to refer to the whole environment, while the word 'windows' refers to application or document windows. There are two types of windows that can appear on your screen; 'applications' windows which contain running applications, and 'document' windows which appear with applications that can open more than one document (we will see an example of this shortly), but share the application window's menu.

Windows makes use of three types of icons; 'application icons' which only appear at the bottom of your screen after you choose to minimise that application, 'document icons' which appear at the bottom of the application window when you minimise that document (for example, the Games icons in the previous screen dump), and 'program icons' which are the icons that appear within a group window in the Program Manager application (for example, those in the Main group of the previous screen dump).

The icons within the Main group have the following function:

Program icon	Function
File Manager	Performs file related operations
Control Panel	Changes system configuration
Print Manager	Manages printing operations
Clipboard/Clipbook	Transfers data between windows
MS-DOS Prompt	Allows temporary exit to DOS

Windows Setup	Calls SETUP to add or remove applications
PIF Editor	Allows you to edit DOS applications start-up files.
Read Me	Contains last minute information not available in the printed documentation
Sysedit	Allows you to edit system files - not always available.

The document icons which appear at the bottom of the Program Manager window have the following function:

Document icon	*Function*
StartUp	Allows you to specify which application is to be loaded on starting up Windows.
Accessories	Contains the applications Write, Paintbrush, Terminal, Notepad, Recorder, Cardfile, Calendar, Calculator, Clock, Object Packager, Character Map, Media Player, and Sound Recorder.
Network	Allows you to set up network applications, such as Mail.
Mouse	Accesses the Mouse Manager (Windows 3.11 only), which allows you to change, amongst other things, the pointer size.
Games	Contains games, namely, Solitaire, Minesweeper, and Reversi or Hearts.
Applications	Contains applications found during installation.

The Mouse Pointers

In Windows, as with all other graphical based programs, the use of a mouse makes many operations both easier and more fun to carry out.

Windows has several different mouse pointers, as illustrated below, which it uses for its various functions. When the program is initially started up the first you will see is the hourglass, which turns into an upward pointing hollow arrow once the Program Manager opens on your screen. Other shapes depend on the type of work you are doing at the time.

The hourglass which displays when you are waiting while performing a function.

The arrow which appears when the pointer is placed over menus, scrolling bars, and buttons.

The I-beam which appears in normal text areas of the screen.

The large 4-headed arrow which appears after choosing the **Control, Move/Size** command(s) for moving or sizing windows.

The double arrows which appear when over the border of a window, used to drag the side and alter the size of the window.

The Help hand which appears in the help windows, and is used to access 'hypertext' type links.

Windows applications, such as word processors, spreadsheets and databases, can have additional mouse pointers which facilitate the execution of selected commands, such as highlighting text, defining areas for the appearance of charts, etc.

Parts of a Window

Each application and some documents you choose to work with open and use separate windows to run in. In order to illustrate the various parts of the Windows screen, we chose to run the File Manager program which is to be found within the Main group of programs. If you would like to see the same thing on your screen, first double-click the File Manager icon, shown here, then select the drive on which Windows is installed (in our case drive C:) by clicking the appropriate drive icon in the File Manager's window, which is to be found below the Tool Bar, then click the WINDOWS directory on the installed drive.

Although every window has some common elements, not all windows use all of these elements.

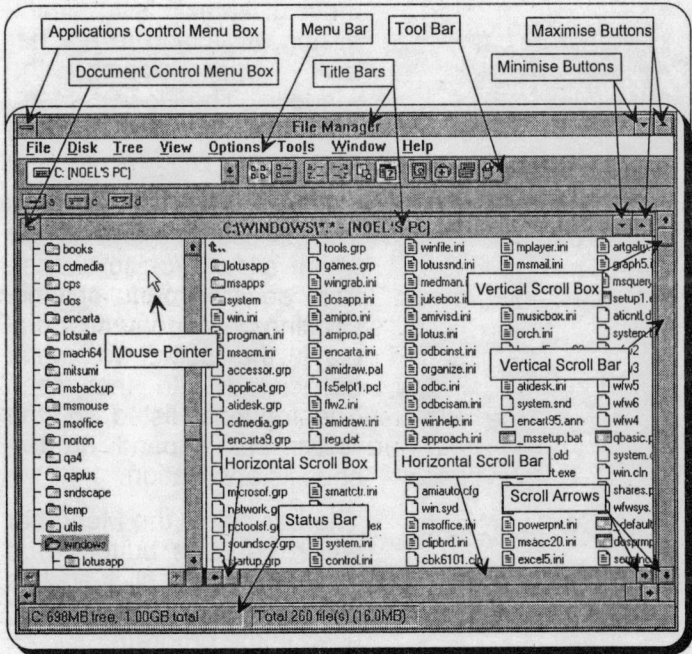

11

Although multiple windows can be displayed simultaneously, only one is the active window (which displays at the top of any other nonactive window). Title bars of nonactive windows appear a lighter shade than those of the active ones.

The Windows screen is subdivided into several areas which have the following functions. These are described from the top of the screen, working from left to right.

Area	*Function*
Control menu boxes	Clicking on the top menu box (upper-left corner of the window), displays the pull-down Control menu which can be used to control the program window. It includes commands for re-sizing, moving, maximising, minimising, switching to another task, and closing the window. The lower menu box controls the current document window in the same manner.
Menu bar	The bar below the Title bar which allows you to choose from several menu options. Clicking on a menu item displays the pull-down menu associated with that item. The options listed in the Menu bar depend on the specific application.
Tool Bar	The bar below the Menu bar which contains buttons that give you mouse click access to the functions most often used in the program.

Maximise button	The button you point to and click to fill the screen with the active window. When that happens, the Maximise button changes to a Restore (vertical double-headed) arrow which can be used to restore the window to its former size.
Minimise box	The button you point to and click to store an application as a small symbol at the bottom of the screen. Double clicking on such an icon will restore the screen.
Title bar	The bar at the top of a window which displays the application name and the name of the current document.
Scroll boxes	The boxes on the Scroll bars that indicate the relative position of the visible part of the document with respect to the whole.
Mouse pointer	The arrow which appears when the pointer is placed over menus, scrolling bars, buttons, and directory lists.
Scroll bars	The bars on the extreme right and bottom of each window that contain a scroll box. Clicking on these bars allows you to see parts of a document that might not be visible in that size window.

Scroll arrows	The arrowheads at each end of each scroll bar at which you can click to scroll the screen up and down one line, or left and right one character, at a time.
Status bar	The area at the lower-left corner of a window in which the current program status and present process is displayed

The Menu Bar Options:

Each window's menu bar option has associated with it a pull-down sub-menu, with the Control menu common to all applications. To activate the menu of a window, either press the <Alt> key, which causes the first option of the menu (in this case **File**) to be highlighted, then use the right and left arrow keys to highlight any of the options in the menu, or use the mouse to point to an option. Pressing either the <Enter> key, or the left mouse button, reveals the pull-down sub-menu of the highlighted menu option.

The sub-menu of the **File** option of the File Manager's window, is shown below.

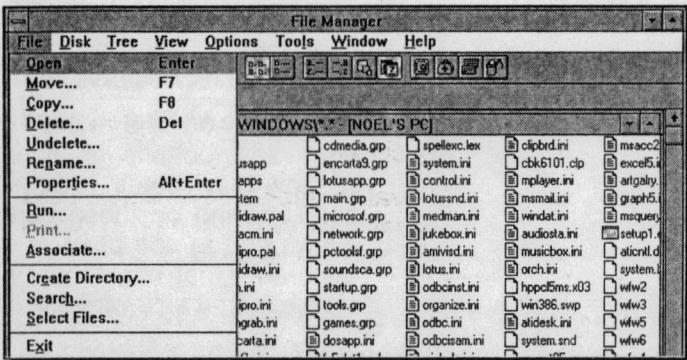

Menu options can also be activated directly by pressing the <Alt> key followed by the underlined letter of the required option. Thus pressing **Alt+F**, causes the pull-down sub-menu of **F**ile to be displayed. You can use the up and down arrow keys to move the highlighted bar up and down a sub-menu, or the right and left arrow keys to move along the options in the menu bar. Pressing the <Enter> key selects the highlighted option or executes the highlighted command. Pressing the <Esc> key once, closes the pull-down sub-menu, while pressing the <Esc> key for a second time, closes the menu system.

The items on the menu bar of a specific application might be different from the ones shown here. However, almost all applications offer the following options:

File   Produces a pull-down menu of mainly file related tasks, which allow you, amongst other tasks, to 'open' a selected item, 'move' a selected item, 'copy' selected files and directories, 'delete' selected files and directories, 'undelete' previously deleted files, 'run' a program by entering its name from the keyboard, and 'exit' the program.

Window   Allows you to 'open' a new window, display multiple windows on your screen in 'cascade' or 'tile' form, or 'arrange icons' within an active window in a pre-determined spacing.

Help   Activates the help window and displays an 'index' of help or offers help on selected topics.

For a more detailed description of each sub-menu item, either highlight it and read the text on the status bar, or use the on-line **H**elp system.

Dialogue Boxes

Three periods after a sub-menu option or command, means that a dialogue box will open when the option or command is selected. A dialogue box is used for the insertion of additional information, such as the name of a file.

To see a dialogue box, first point and click (once) on the **win.ini** file which is to be found in the \WINDOWS directory, then click once on the File Manager's **File** menu option, and select the **Properties** sub-menu. The Properties dialogue box appears on the screen, as shown below:

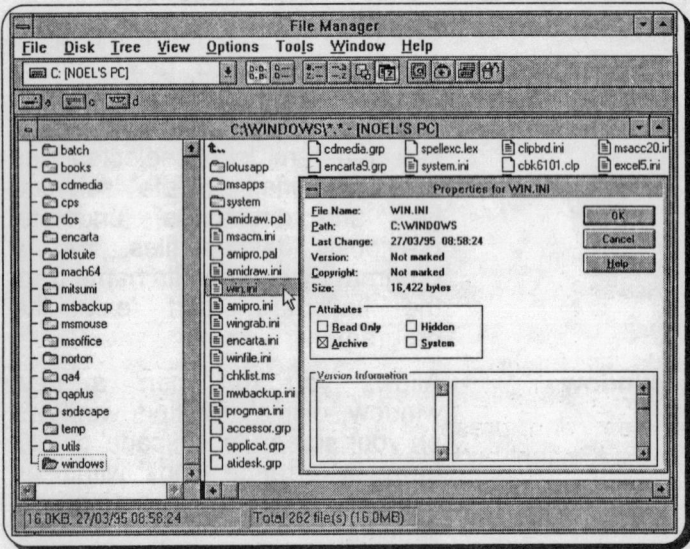

When a dialogue box opens, the <Tab> key can be used to move the cursor from one field to another (Shift+<Tab> moves the cursor backwards) or alternatively you can move directly to a desired field by holding the <Alt> key down and pressing the underlined letter in the field name.

Within a group of options you can use the arrow keys to move from one option to another. Having selected an option or typed in information, you must press a command button, such as the **OK** or **Cancel** button, or choose from additional options. To select the **OK** button with the mouse, simply point and click, while with the keyboard, you must first press the <Tab> key until the dotted rectangle moves to the required button, and then press the <Enter> key.

Some dialogue boxes contain 'List' boxes which show a column of available choices, as shown below.

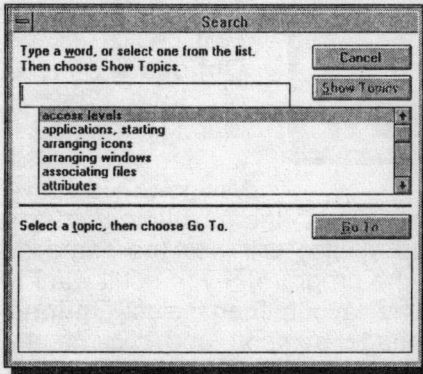

This dialogue box was obtained by clicking on File Manager's **Help** menu option and then selecting the **Search for Help on** sub-menu.

If there are more choices than can be seen in the area provided, use the scroll bars to reveal them. To select a single item from a List box, either double-click the item, or use the arrow keys to highlight the item and press <Enter>. Other dialogue boxes contain 'Option' buttons with a list of mutually exclusive items. The default choice is marked with a black dot against its name, while unavailable options are dimmed. Another type of dialogue box contains 'Check' boxes which offer a list of options you can switch on or off. Selected options show a cross in the box against the option name.

To cancel a dialogue box, either press the **Cancel** button, or the <Esc> key. Pressing the <Esc> key in succession, closes one dialogue box at a time, and eventually aborts the menu option.

17

Ending a Windows Session

To end a Windows session, select the **Exit Windows** command from the Program Manager's **File** menu, or the Control menu. However, before doing so, make sure you first close the applications you are running so as not to lose the latest changes to your work.

No matter which method you choose to quit Windows, Program Manager always asks you to confirm your request with the following Exit Windows dialogue box:

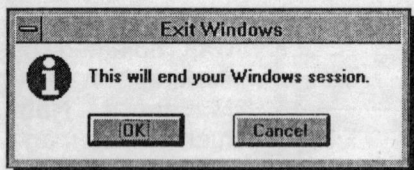

By default, the **Save Settings on Exit** choice, in the **Options** sub-menu of the Program Manager's window, is set to cause Windows to save the current display layout. Thus, the next time you start Windows, your desktop display will look the same as the last time you used the program. If you don't want to save the current display layout, then select **Options** from the Program Manager's menu and click at the **Save Settings on Exit** option to remove the tick mark against this sub-menu choice. From now on, this becomes the new default state for the Exit Windows dialogue box, until you decide to change it again.

3. THE WINDOWS ENVIRONMENT

Windows allows the display of multiple applications or multiple documents of a single application, if your computer's processor is an 80386, or higher. Each of these Windows applications or documents, displays on the screen in its own window, which can be full screen size, part screen size, or reduced to an icon. Further, document windows of a single application can be tiled or cascaded on the screen for easy access.

Manipulating Windows

To use any Windows program effectively, you will need to be able to manipulate a series of windows, to select which one is to be active, to move them, or change their size, so that you can see all the relevant parts of each one. What follows is a short discussion on how to manipulate windows.

To help with the illustration of the various points to be discussed shortly, we will create three windows in the File Manager program. To do this, double-click on the File Manager icon, shown here, which can be found in the Windows Program Manager's Main group of programs.

If you have used the File Manager as suggested in Chapter 2, what displays on your screen is shown overleaf. The screen dump is a composite, showing the File Manager's screen with the **View** pull-down menu open to show the selected viewing settings, which are shown ticked. The first of these settings is important, as it allows you to see both the directory tree and the files under the selected directory in their individual panes.

On the same screen dump, we show the **Window** pull-down menu open so that you can see what to do next. These two menu options can not be selected simultaneously, but we use this facility to avoid almost duplicate screen dumps, thus saving book space.

19

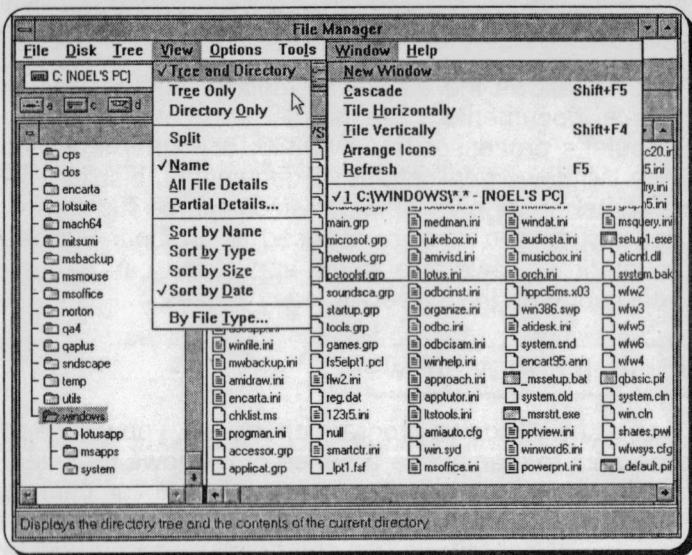

Next, select the **New Window** sub-menu option twice. What you should have on your screen is:

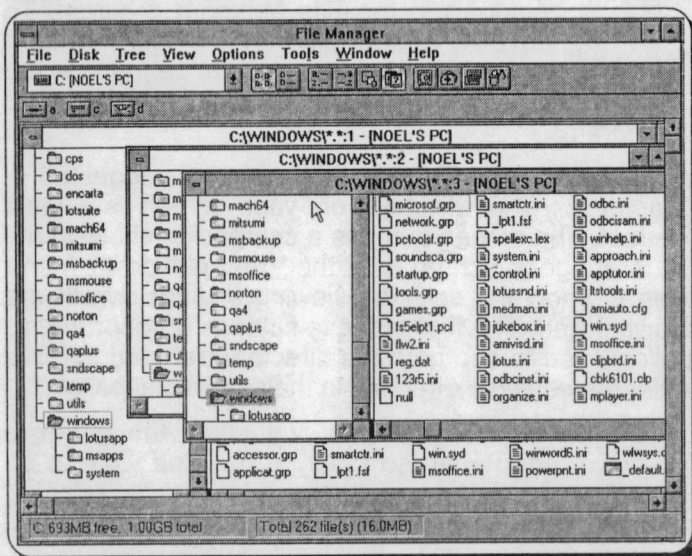

Changing the Active Window:

To select the active window amongst those displayed on the screen, point to it and click the left mouse button, or, if you are in full screen mode, choose the **Window** option of the main menu and select the appropriate number of the window you want to make the active one.

It is a good idea to practise what we are describing here by using the three newly created File Manager's windows. Do not be afraid if you make mistakes - the more mistakes you make the more you will learn!

Moving Windows and Dialogue Boxes:

When you have multiple windows or dialogue boxes on the screen, you might want to move a particular one to a different part of the screen. This can be achieved with either the mouse or the keyboard, but not if the window occupies the full screen, for obvious reasons.

To move a window, or a dialogue box, with the mouse, point to the title bar and drag it (press the left button and keep it pressed while moving the mouse) until the shadow border is where you want it to be (as shown below), then release the mouse button.

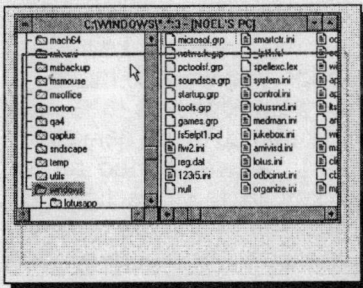

To move a window with the keyboard, press <Alt+Spacebar> to reveal the Application Control menu, or <Alt+–> to reveal the Document Control menu. Then, press **M** to select **M**ove which causes a four-headed arrow to appear in the title bar and use the arrow keys to move the shadow border of the window to the required place. Press <Enter> to fix the window to its new position or <Esc> to cancel the relocation.

Sizing a Window:

You can change the size of a window with either the mouse or the keyboard.

To size an active window with the mouse, move the window so that the side you want to change is visible, then move the mouse pointer to the edge of the window or corner so that it changes to a two-headed arrow, then drag the two-headed arrow in the direction you want that side or corner to move. Below we are moving the left side of the window towards the right, thus making the window smaller. Continue dragging until the shadow border is the size you require, then release the mouse button.

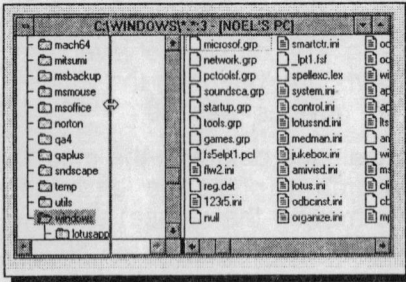

To size a window with the keyboard, press either <Alt+Spacebar> or <Alt+–> to reveal the Application Control menu or the Document Control menu, then press **S** to select **S**ize which causes the four-headed arrow to appear, as shown here. Now press the arrow key that corresponds to the edge you want to move, or if a corner, press the two arrow keys (one after the other) corresponding to the particular corner, which causes the pointer to change to a two-headed arrow. Press an appropriate arrow key in the direction you want that side or corner to move and continue to do so until the shadow border is the size you require, then press <Enter> to fix the new window size.

Minimising and Maximising Windows:

A document window (or an application) can be minimised into an icon at the bottom of the screen. This can be done either by using the mouse to click the 'Minimise' button (the downward arrow in the upper-right corner of the window), or by pressing <Alt+Spacebar> or <Alt+−> to reveal the Application Control menu or the Document Control menu, and selecting **n** for **Mi̱nimise**.

In the above screen dump we show windows 2 and 3 minimised at the bottom of the screen and the mouse pointer pointing at the minimise button of window 1.

To maximise a window so that it fills the entire screen, either click on the 'maximise' button (the upward arrow in the upper-right corner of the window), or press <Alt+Spacebar> or <Alt+−> to display the Application Control menu or the Document Control menu, and select **x** for **Ma̱ximise**.

An application which has been minimised or maximised can be returned to its original size and position on the screen by either double-clicking on its icon to expand it to a window, or clicking on the double-headed button in the upper-right corner of the maximised window, shown here, to reduce it to its former size.

With the keyboard, press <Alt+Spacebar> to display the Application Control menu, or <Alt+−> to display the Document Control menu, and select **R** for **Ṟestore**.

23

Closing a Window:

A document window can be closed at any time to save screen space and memory. To do this, either double-click on the Control menu button (the large hyphen in the upper-left corner of the window, or press <Alt+−> and select **C** for **Close** from the Control menu.

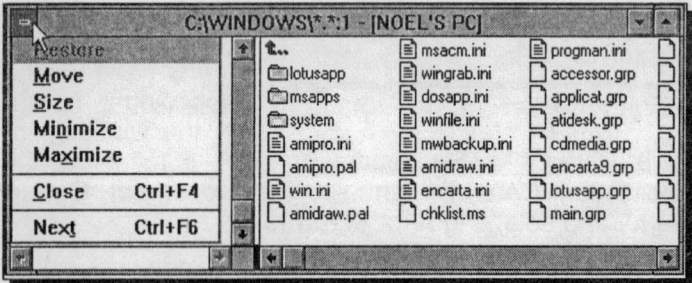

If you try to close a window of an application document, such as that of a word processor, in which you have made changes since the last time you saved it, you will get a warning in the form of a dialogue box asking confirmation prior to closing it. This safeguards against loss of information.

Windows Display Arrangement:

In Windows and most Windows application programs, you can display multiple windows in both tiled and cascaded (overlapping) forms - the choice being a matter of balance between personal preference and the type of work you are doing at the time.

On the next page we show the two forms of windows display side-by-side. Again, these two screen dumps are shown together to conserve space. You, of course, will only be able to see one at a time, but it will fill the whole of your screen. For the left half of the screen we used the **Cascade** option, while for the right half we used the **Tile Horizontally** option.

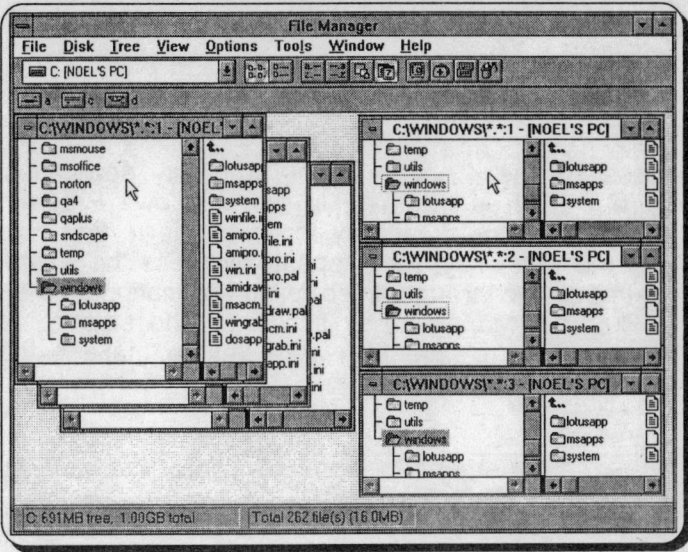

When you are using certain Windows applications, it is very easy to open more files or documents than you need. Unless you check with the **Window** command, as shown here, you may not even know that some of these files or documents are open. Some applications allow you the option of closing the active window (the one whose title bar is highlighted) when a new one is opened.

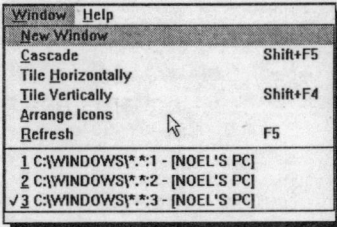

We recommend you check every now and then and, to conserve memory, close any unwanted files or documents, by first making them active, then either using the **File, Close** command, or double-clicking the left mouse button on the document control box. The document control box is at the left end of the menu bar, if the document is set to full page, or at the left end of the document title bar, if it is windowed.

25

The Windows Control Panel

The Control Panel provides a quick and easy way to change the hardware and software settings of your system.

Access to the Control Panel, from an application program involves returning to the Windows Program Manager. The quickest way to do this is to first hold down the <Alt> key, then repeatedly press the <Tab> key; this cycles through any running applications. When the Program Manager box shows on the screen, as shown below, release the <Alt> key to make it the active application.

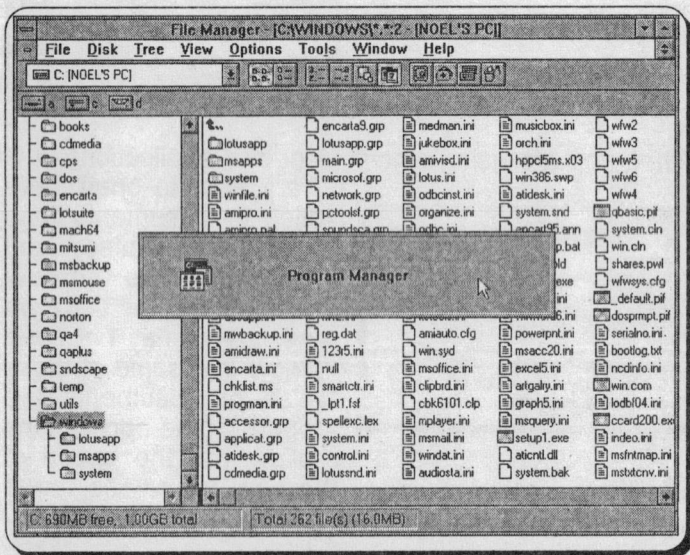

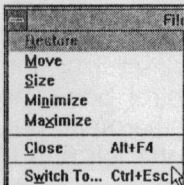

Another way to perform the same application change, makes use of the Application's Control Menu which is opened when the upper Control box is clicked on. Select **Switch To** from this menu, shown here, to open the

Task List dialogue box, shown below. This gives a listing of all the applications that are currently running under Windows. Select the Program Manager option and click on the **Switch To** button.

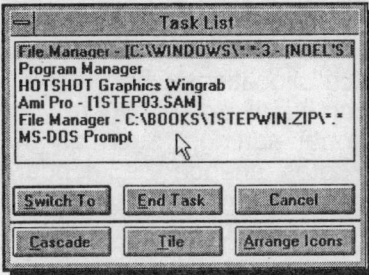

The other buttons in this box allow you to manipulate and close the windows of running applications and to arrange any icons at the bottom of the screen.

Once in the Program Manager window, you can normally find the Control Panel icon, shown here, in the Main group window. Double-clicking on this icon will open the Control Panel window, shown below, from which the various Control Panel options can be accessed.

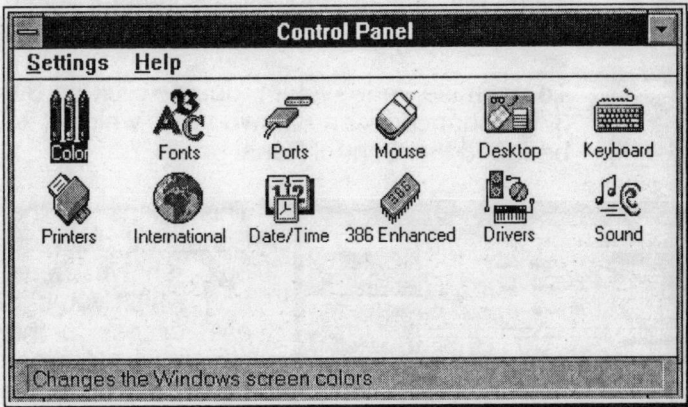

Double-clicking at the Control Panel icons allows you to change the display colours, change the display and printer fonts, and specify parameters for any serial ports installed on your system. Further, you can change the settings of your mouse, change the appearance of your display, and specify resource allocations when running in 386 mode. Finally, you can install and configure your printer(s), specify international settings, such as the formatting of numbers and dates, change the keyboard repeat rate, change the date and time of your system, and specify whether Windows should beep when it detects an error.

All of these features control the environment in which the Windows application programs operate and you should become familiar with them.

Optimising Windows:

If your machine is equipped with a 386, 486 or Pentium processor, you can speed up Windows by using a permanent Swap File - a hidden file on your hard disc which is used for swapping information from memory to the disc. In addition, if you are running Windows 3.11, you have the option of using a 32-bit disc and file access, which will speed up your computer even further.

To optimise your system, double-click on the 386 Enhanced icon, shown here, which is to be found the Control Panel group.

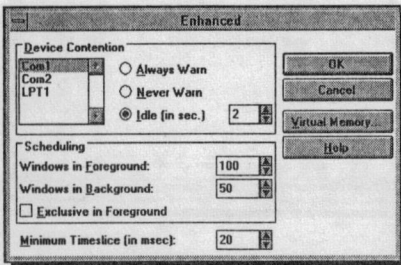

This opens up the Enhanced dialogue box, shown here, from which you can gain access to the Virtual Memory dialogue box by clicking the **Virtual Memory** button.

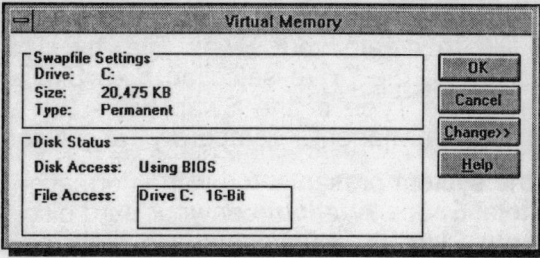

This dialogue box informs you that a Swap File already exists on the C: drive, it is 20MB in size, and is permanent. If you have not set a swap file on your system, then no drive letter would appear against **Drive**, and the numeral zero (0) would appear against **Size**.

To add a Swap File, or change the settings of the current one, click the **Change** button to reveal the Virtual Memory dialogue box, shown below:

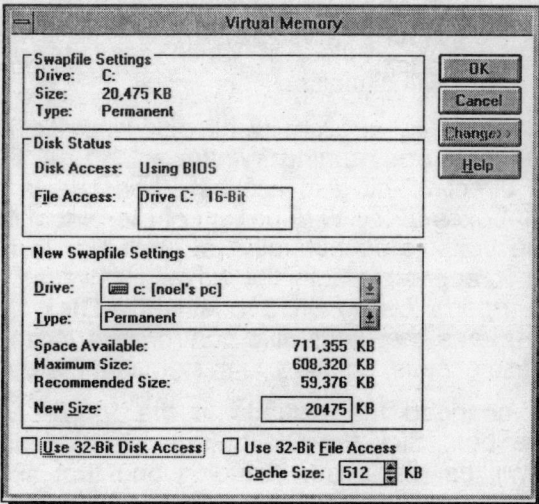

In this dialogue box you can select on which drive you would like to create your Swap File, by clicking the down-arrow of the **Drive** selection box. Similarly, you can select the **Type** of the Swap File - the available types being 'Permanent', 'Temporary', and 'None'.

Next, the system presents you with information relating to the total **Space Available** on your hard disc, and the **Maximum Size** of contiguous space detected on your disc, which can be less than the total space available. A permanent Swap File requires contiguous space on the disc. Finally, the system displays what it thinks should be the **Recommended Size** of your Swap File. This recommendation is usually half the size of the detected maximum size, but you do not have to accept it.

To enter the size *you* would like for the Swap File, change the value in the **New Size** box. If you are creating a Permanent Swap File, this will be the size allocated to it on your hard disc, which cannot be used for any other purpose, until you change its size. If, on the other hand, you are creating a Temporary Swap File, this is the maximum size that the Swap File can grow to, but the space allocated to it can be used by other programs or files, in which case its size and effectiveness will diminish.

If you would like to use 32-bit disc and file access, provided you are running Windows 3.11 (A Pentium uses a direct 32-bit disc access), then check the two relevant boxes at the very bottom of the Virtual Memory dialogue box. To do this, click at each box in turn, so that an X appears within the boxes. However, if your system reports *'Using BIOS'* against the **Disk Access:** then it means that your disc controller is incapable of 32-bit disc access, unless you system is a Pentium.

Having changed the settings in the Virtual Memory dialogue box, click the **OK** button. Warning dialogue boxes will be displayed, including one that asks you whether you would like the changes to take effect now by restarting Windows. If you don't restart Windows **now**, none of your changes will take effect.

4. CONTROLLING INFORMATION

When you are using Windows or one of its applications, you will invariably come across a **Read Me** or **Update Notes** icon which contains last minute information not available in printed form in the User Guides. To enable you to read such information, vendors use either the Write or the Notepad Accessory. What follows, will show you how to read such files, print them, or copy them onto the Clipboard/Clipbook, so that you can transfer the information into another package.

Microsoft's Write

The Windows Write icon, when used by different vendors, might have a different caption than the one shown here. If you cannot locate this icon (found in the Program Manager's Main group under Windows 3.11), use another visually similar 'pen' icon. You can even use the Microsoft Write icon itself, to be found in the Accessories group. Double-clicking on such an icon displays the following screen:

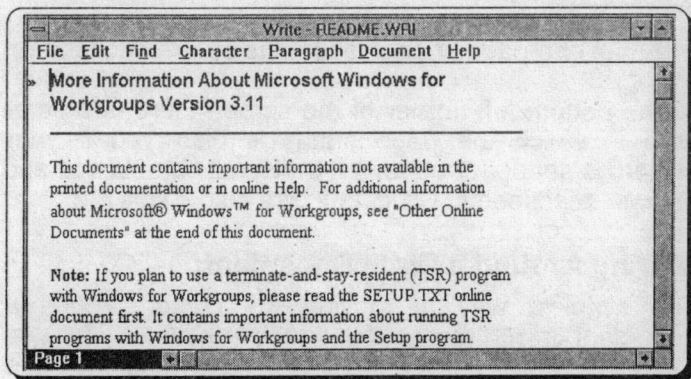

```
═                      Write - README.WRI                        ▼ ▲
 File  Edit  Find   Character   Paragraph  Document   Help
▶  More Information About Microsoft Windows for
    Workgroups Version 3.11
    ─────────────────────────────────────────────────
    This document contains important information not available in the
    printed documentation or in online Help.  For additional information
    about Microsoft® Windows™ for Workgroups, see "Other Online
    Documents" at the end of this document.

    Note: If you plan to use a terminate-and-stay-resident (TSR) program
    with Windows for Workgroups, please read the SETUP.TXT online
    document first. It contains important information about running TSR
    programs with Windows for Workgroups and the Setup program.
 Page 1         ▼                                               ▼
```

If you were using the Microsoft Write icon from the Accessories group, the screen will be the same, but empty; there will be no text associated with it.

The Write Screen:

The top line of the Write screen is the 'Title' bar which contains the name of the document, and if this bar is dragged with the mouse the window can be moved around the screen. Also, just like any other window, its size can be changed by dragging any of its four sides in the required direction.

The second line of the screen displays the 'Menu' bar which allows access to the following sub menus:

File Edit Find Character Paragraph Document Help

As described in Chapter 2 - 'Starting Windows' - the sub-menus are accessed either with your mouse, or by pressing the <Alt> key followed by the underlined letter.

In a Write document you will notice three marks which appear in the working area of the screen. These are:

| the blinking vertical line indicating the text insertion point.

¤ the end mark which identifies the end of a document.

» the page mark which identifies the beginning of a page, if pagination has been switched on.

At the bottom left corner of the screen there is a small area in which the page status is displayed If your system is set up for a mouse, the scroll bars, boxes and arrows, described in Chapter 2, are also displayed.

Moving Around a Write Document:

The simplest way of moving the cursor around a document is with the normal direction keys (←, ↑, →, ↓, Page Up, Page Down), or if you have paginated the document, with the **Find, Go To Page** command, which allows you to jump to a specified page number. If you have a mouse, click on the arrow buttons on the scroll bars, or on the scroll bars themselves for larger shifts.

Microsoft's Notepad

Notepad is a text editor (not as powerful as Write) which can only be used to read smallish text files such as the various .TXT files supplied with Windows. Some software vendors supply last minute information using the Notepad editor. As with Write, if you cannot locate this particular icon, use another visually similar 'notepad' icon, irrespective of the caption. You can even use the Microsoft Notepad icon itself, to be found in the Accessories group. Double-clicking on such an icon displays the following screen:

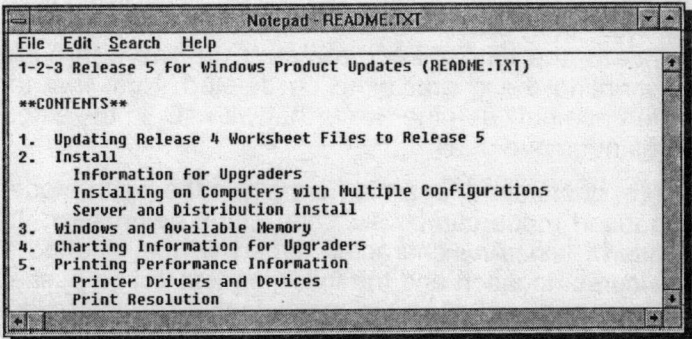

```
┌──────────────────────────────────────────────────────┐
│ ─              Notepad - README.TXT              ▼ ▲  │
├──────────────────────────────────────────────────────┤
│ File  Edit  Search  Help                             │
├──────────────────────────────────────────────────────┤
│ 1-2-3 Release 5 For Windows Product Updates (README.TXT) ▲│
│                                                       │
│ **CONTENTS**                                          │
│                                                       │
│ 1.  Updating Release 4 Worksheet Files to Release 5  │
│ 2.  Install                                          │
│       Information for Upgraders                       │
│       Installing on Computers with Multiple Configurations│
│       Server and Distribution Install                │
│ 3.  Windows and Available Memory                     │
│ 4.  Charting Information for Upgraders               │
│ 5.  Printing Performance Information                 │
│       Printer Drivers and Devices                    │
│       Print Resolution                             ▼ │
│ ◄                                                  ► │
└──────────────────────────────────────────────────────┘
```

As with Write, if you were using the Microsoft Notepad icon from the Accessories group, the screen will be the same, but empty; there will be no text associated with it.

Moving Around a Notepad Document:

As with Write, the simplest way of moving the cursor around a Notepad document is with the normal direction keys (←, ↑, →, ↓, Page Up, Page Down). However, a Notepad document cannot be paginated and, therefore, you cannot jump to a specific page. If you have a mouse, click on the arrow buttons on the scroll bars, or on the scroll bars themselves for larger shifts.

Document Editing

You might need to edit an existing Write or Notepad document, because you intend to use it in a different form somewhere else. This could include deleting unwanted words, correcting a mistake or adding extra text. All these operations are very easy to carry out.

For small deletions, such as letters or words, the easiest method to adopt is the use of the <Del> or <BkSp> keys. With the <Del> key, position the cursor on the first letter you want to delete and press <Del>; the letter is deleted and the following text moves one space to the left. With the <BkSp> key, position the cursor immediately to the right of the character to be deleted and press <BkSp>; the cursor moves one space to the left pulling the rest of the line with it and overwriting the character to be deleted. Note that the difference between the two is that with <Del> the cursor does not move at all.

Write, or Notepad, operate normally in the insert mode - the insert mode can be switched off/on by pressing the <Insert> key. Any characters typed will be inserted at the cursor location and the following text will be pushed to the right, and down, to make room. To insert blank lines in your text, place the cursor at the beginning of the line where the blank is needed and press <Enter>. To remove the blank line position the cursor at its leftmost end and press <Del>.

Edit	Find	Character
Undo		Ctrl+Z
Cut		Ctrl+X
Copy		Ctrl+C
Paste		Ctrl+V
Paste Special...		
Paste Link		
Links...		
Object		
Insert Object...		
Move Picture		
Size Picture		

When larger scale editing is needed, use the **Cut, Copy** and **Paste** operations. However, the text to be altered must be 'selected' before the operation can be carried out. These functions are then available when the **Edit** sub-menu is activated, as shown here. This sub-menu will be displayed if you are using Write. With Notepad the sub-menu is slightly simpler.

Selecting Text:

The procedure in Write, or Notepad, before any operation such as editing can be carried out on text, is first to select the text to be altered. Selected text is highlighted on the screen. This can be carried out in several ways:

   a. Using the keyboard; position the cursor on the first character to be selected and hold down the <Shift> key while using the direction keys to highlight the required text, then release the <Shift> key. Navigational key combinations can be used with the <Shift> key to highlight blocks of text. For example, to highlight the text from the present cursor position to the end of the line, use <Shift+End>, while to highlight the text from the present cursor position to the end of the document, use <Shift+Ctrl+End>.

   b. With the mouse; click the left mouse button at the beginning of the block and drag the cursor across the block so that the desired text is highlighted, then release the mouse button. To select a word, double-click at the word, to select a block, place the cursor at the beginning of the block, press the <Shift> key down and while holding it pressed, move the mouse pointer to the end of the desired block, and click the left mouse button.

Copying, Moving, & Deleting Blocks of Text:

Once text has been selected it can be copied to another location in your present document, to another Write or Notepad document, or even to another Windows application. To do this, use either the **Edit, Copy** command sequence from the menu, moving the cursor to the start of where you want the copied text, then use the **Edit, Paste** command, or use the quick key combination - <Ctrl+C> to copy and <Ctrl+V> to paste, which does not require the menu bar to be activated.

Selected text can be moved to any location in the same document. To move text, select it, then use either the **Edit, Cut,** command, move the cursor to the required new location and use the **Edit, Paste** command, or use the quick key combination <Ctrl+X> to cut and <Ctrl+V> to paste. The moved text will be placed at the cursor location and will force any existing text to make room for it. This operation can be cancelled by simply pressing <Esc>.

When text is deleted it is removed from the document. With Write any selected text can be deleted by pressing **Edit, Cut,** or by simply pressing the <Del> key. However, using **Edit, Cut**, allows you to use the **Edit, Paste** command, while using the <Del> key, does not.

The Undo Command:

As text is lost with the delete command you should use it with caution, but if you do make a mistake all is not lost as long as you act immediately. The **Edit, Undo** command reverses your most recent editing or formatting command, so you need to use it before carrying out any further operations. The quick key for this command is <Ctrl+Z>.

Page Breaks:

In Write only, the program automatically inserts a page break in a document when a page of typed text is full and the **File, Repaginate** command has been used. When Write inserts a page break automatically, it prevents a single line in a paragraph from being printed by itself at the top or bottom of a page.

To force a manual page break in a document, use the key combination <Ctrl+Enter>. The resulting page break symbol in this case is a complete row of dots and Write readjusts all the non-manual page breaks for the remainder of the document. Manual page breaks can be selected, deleted, or copied.

Printing Documents

When Windows was first installed on your computer the printers you intend to use should have been selected, which would have caused the SETUP program to copy the appropriate printer drivers from the distribution discs. Before printing for the first time, it is essential to ensure that your printer is properly installed (see Chapter 7).

If you want to produce high-quality documents, and you have access to a laser printer (even if not connected to your computer), then use the **File, Print Setup** command, which displays the dialogue box shown below, to install the laser printer as an additional printer to be used with Windows and configure it to print to 'File'.

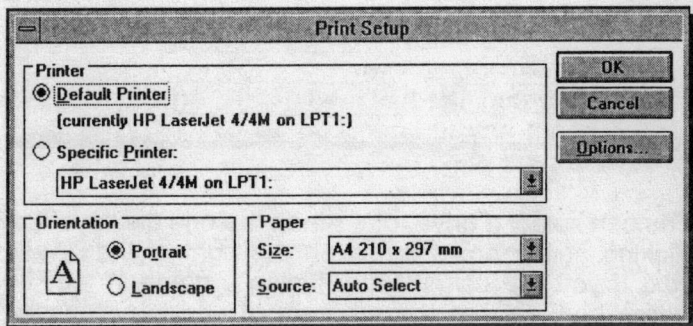

	Print Setup	
Printer		OK
◉ Default Printer		Cancel
(currently HP LaserJet 4/4M on LPT1:)		
○ Specific Printer:		Options...
HP LaserJet 4/4M on LPT1:	⬥	
Orientation	**Paper**	
◉ Portrait	Size: A4 210 x 297 mm ⬥	
○ Landscape	Source: Auto Select ⬥	

From this dialogue box you can select the **Orientation** of the printed page, and the **Paper Size**. Next, use the **File, Print** command, to send your document to either the printer connected to your computer or to an encoded file on disc.

Do remember that, when using Microsoft's Write and you change printers, the appearance of your document might change as the program uses the fonts available with the newly selected printer. This can affect the line lengths, which in turn will affect tabulation and page breaks.

37

Saving a Changed Document

To save a document, use the **File, Save As** command. A dialogue box appears on the screen, as shown below, with the cursor in the **File Name** box waiting for you to type a name; it must not be more than 8 alphanumeric characters in length, and it must not contain any spaces or punctuation.

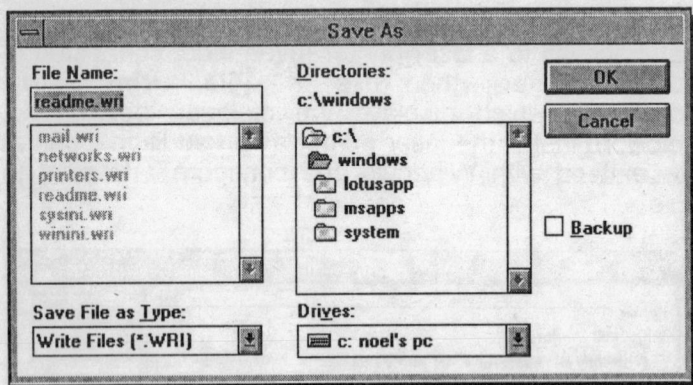

You can select a drive, other than the one displayed, by clicking at the down arrow on the right of the **Drives** box. If you are using Write, typing a name in the **File Name** box, causes the program to add the extension WRI, automatically to the filename. In the case of Notepad, the automatic file extension is TXT.

In Write you can save a document with six different extensions. The most important of these are:

Write Files (*.WRI)	A Write formatted document.
Text Files (*.TXT)	A Windows ANSI file. Use this option if your document is program code or you intend to telecommunicate it.
All Files (*.*)	An unformatted ASCII file.

38

Using the Clipboard/Clipbook

If you are using Windows 3.0 or 3.1, you have access to a Clipboard which is a temporary storage location for information you want to cut or copy. The Clipboard icon, shown here, is to be found in the Program Manager's Main group.

If you are using Windows for Workgroups 3.11, then you have access to a superior tool, called the ClipBook, which incorporates not only the Clipboard, but also a Local ClipBook and a ClipBook Viewer.

The Local ClipBook is a long term storage location for information you want to save, move or share. Each part of information you paste on the Local ClipBook is called a 'page'. A Local ClipBook can be thought of as personal notebook with several pages. Unlike Clipboard, the information you transfer to it, is stored and is safe even after you quit Windows for Workgroups. When you want to use information contained in a page of your Local ClipBook, you copy that page back onto your Clipboard before you paste it into another application.

The ClipBook Viewer is a tool you use to view information on the Clipboard, the Local ClipBook, and if you are using Microsoft's network, the ClipBooks on other connected computers. The ClipBook Viewer icon, shown here, is to be found in the Windows for Workgroups Program Manager's Main group.

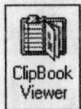

Since the Clipboard is part and parcel of the ClipBook application, the rest of this discussion will be confined to the latter one only. But, if you are using Windows 3.0 or 3.1, you must remember that you can only use the Clipboard part of it; the other facilities of the ClipBook will not be available to you.

In fact we have already used the Clipboard when using the **Cut** and **Paste** features found in Write, and Notepad (and in other Windows word processors).

Apart from cutting, copying and pasting operations in Windows applications, you can also use the Clipboard to copy the contents of an application's window, or to copy Windows graphics images, so that you can transfer such information to other applications. There are two ways of copying information:

- Press the <Print Screen> key to copy onto the Clipboard the contents of a whole Windows screen, even if that screen is a DOS application.

- Press the <Alt+Print Screen> key combination to copy onto the Clipboard the contents of the current open window, or dialogue box.

To illustrate these techniques follow the step-by-step instructions given below.

To Copy a Full Windows Screen:

Return to the Program Manager, and make sure that both the Main and Accessories group windows are open. Then press the <Print Screen> key, and double-click on the Clipboard/ClipBook icon. The following will be displayed:

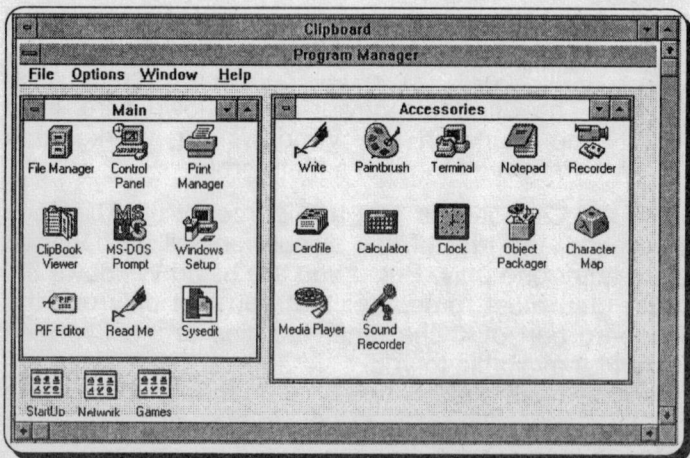

To Copy the Contents of a Current Open Window:

Double-click on the Control Panel icon, shown here, and press the <Alt+Print Screen> keys. Then, double-click on the Clipboard/ClipBook icon. The following will be displayed:

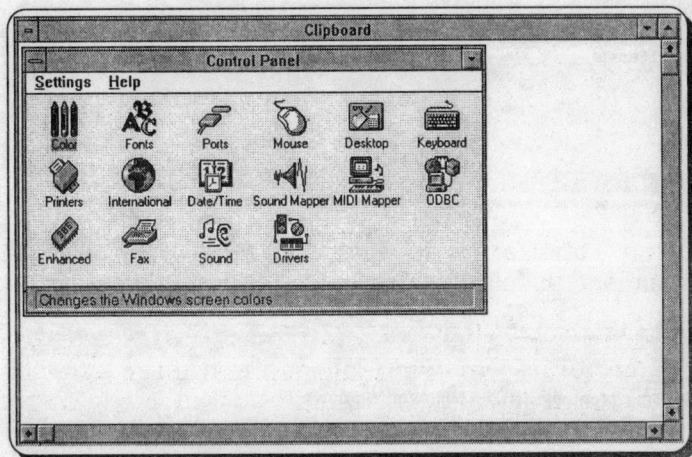

To copy a DOS screen:

Double-click the DOS Prompt icon, shown here, then type

```
type c:\config.sys
```

and press <Enter> to display the contents of your configuration file. Next press the <Print Screen> key, and double-click on the Clipboard/ ClipBook icon. The screen shown on the next page will be displayed.

Having clicked at the DOS Prompt icon, we could have loaded a DOS application and used the above method to capture a screen of such an application. The example we used above is slightly simpler.

```
Clipboard

C:\>type config.sys
SHELL=C:\COMMAND.COM C:\ /P /E:512
DEVICE=C:\DOS\HIMEM.SYS
COUNTRY=044,,C:\DOS\COUNTRY.SYS
DEVICE=C:\DOS\SETVER.EXE
DEVICE=C:\DOS\EMM386.EXE NOEMS X=F000-F7FF
DEVICEHIGH=C:\DOS\POWER.EXE
DEVICEHIGH=C:\WINDOWS\IFSHLP.SYS
DEVICE=C:\DOS\ANSI.SYS
DOS=HIGH,UMB
STACKS=9,256
FILES=50
DEVICEHIGH=C:\Mitsumi\MTMCDAI.SYS /D:MTMIDE01 /P:170,15
BUFFERS=10


C:\>
```

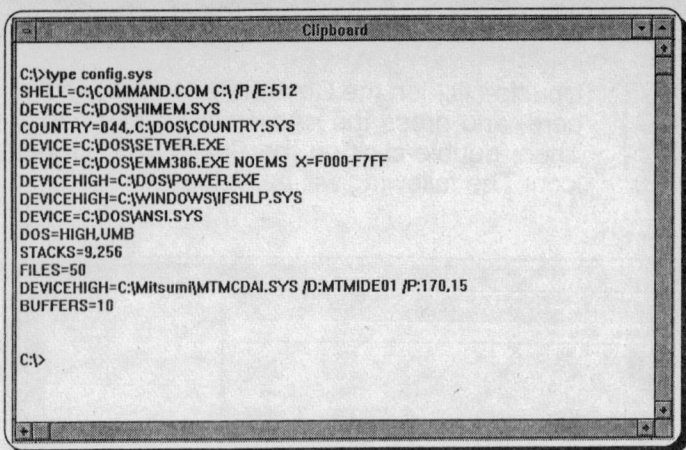

As an exercise, try to date and time stamp a Write document, as follows:

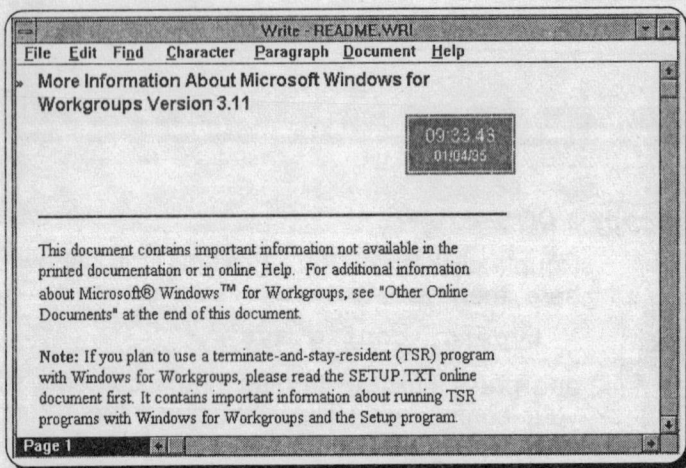

```
Write - README.WRI

File   Edit   Find   Character   Paragraph   Document   Help

» More Information About Microsoft Windows for
  Workgroups Version 3.11
                                        09:33.46
                                        01/04/95



  This document contains important information not available in the
  printed documentation or in online Help.  For additional information
  about Microsoft® Windows™ for Workgroups, see "Other Online
  Documents" at the end of this document.

  Note: If you plan to use a terminate-and-stay-resident (TSR) program
  with Windows for Workgroups, please read the SETUP.TXT online
  document first. It contains important information about running TSR
  programs with Windows for Workgroups and the Setup program.

Page 1
```

To achieve the above, double-click the Clock icon in the Accessories group, then use the **Settings, Digital**, **No Title** commands to obtain the type of clock shown above. Next, size it, capture it with <Alt+Print Screen>, paste it into Write, and use the **Edit, Move Picture** command to position it.

Using the ClipBook Viewer:

The ClipBook Viewer has two windows - one for the Clipboard which displays its current contents, and one for the Local ClipBook which displays the contents stored in it.

If you press <Print Screen> after the previous exercise, double-clicking on the ClipBook Viewer icon, displays something like the following:

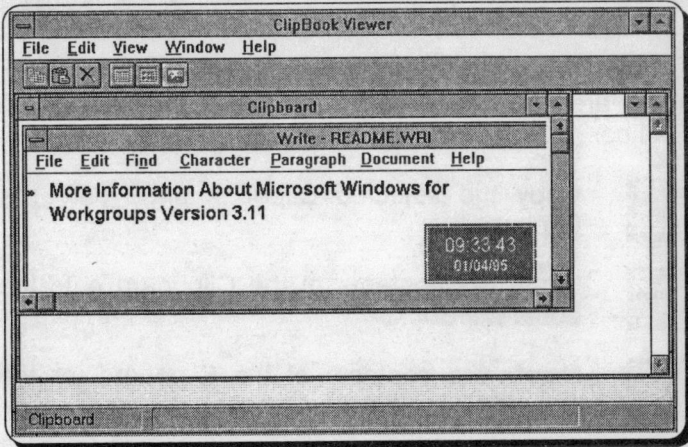

As you can see, the Clipboard contains the Write document with the Clock picture superimposed on it, while immediately behind the Clipboard window you see another window which is the first page of the Local ClipBook.

To switch from the Clipboard to the Local ClipBook window, either click on that part of the ClipBook window visible to you, or use the **Window, 2 Local ClipBook** command, as shown here.

Saving the Contents of the Clipboard:

The contents of the Clipboard can either be saved in the Local ClipBook, or as a file (with the .CLP extension). The advantage of saving on the Local Clipboard is that information is more accessible to you, and others if you are connected to a local network.

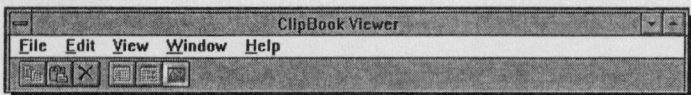

The ClipBook's Menu bar supports the usual options, which are self explanatory. However, the icons on the Tool bar require some explanation.

Copy the selected ClipBook page onto the Clipboard.

Paste the contents of the Clipboard onto the Local ClipBook.

Delete the contents of the Clipboard, or the selected Local ClipBook page.

Display the titles of the pages saved on the ClipBook in a Table of Contents.

Display small pictures (thumbnails) of each page on the ClipBook.

Display the contents of the selected page on a ClipBook.

If you are networked, the Tool bar will show four additional icons which are displayed first. They can be used to 'Connect', 'Disconnect', 'Share', and 'Stop Sharing' the ClipBook with others.

Try to save several different pages on the ClipBook, and explore its unique capabilities.

5. THE FILE MANAGER

To start the File Manager, double-click at its icon, shown here, which is to be found in the Program Manager's Main group. On starting File Manager its split window fills the screen with the 'directory tree' appearing on the left, and the 'lists of files' on the right. The appearance of the directory tree will depend on which **Tree** sub-menu options you have selected from the File Manager's menu bar. For example, selecting **Collapse Branch** and **Indicate Expandable Branches**, displays the following screen:

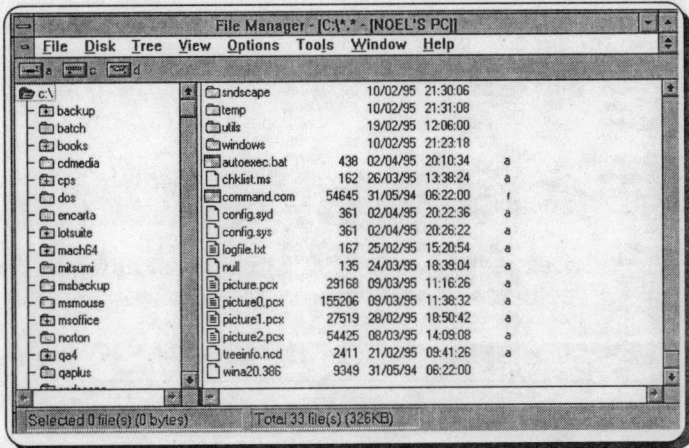

```
File Manager - [C:\*.* - [NOEL'S PC]]
 File   Disk   Tree   View   Options   Tools   Window   Help

 a    c    d

 c:\                    sndscape          10/02/95  21:30:06
   backup               temp              10/02/95  21:31:08
   batch                utils             19/02/95  12:06:00
   books                windows           10/02/95  21:23:18
   cdmedia              autoexec.bat  438 02/04/95  20:10:34   a
   cps                  chklist.ms    162 26/03/95  13:38:24   a
   dos                  command.com 54645 31/05/94  06:22:00   f
   encarta              config.syd    361 02/04/95  20:22:36   a
   lotsuite             config.sys    361 02/04/95  20:26:22   a
   mach64               logfile.txt   167 25/02/95  15:20:54   a
   mitsumi              null          135 24/03/95  18:39:04   a
   msbackup             picture.pcx 29168 09/03/95  11:16:26   a
   msmouse              picture0.pcx 155206 09/03/95 11:38:32  a
   msoffice             picture1.pcx 27519 28/02/95 18:50:42   a
   norton               picture2.pcx 54425 08/03/95 14:09:08   a
   qa4                  treeinfo.ncd 2411 21/02/95  09:41:26   a
   qaplus               wina20.386   9349 31/05/94  06:22:00

 Selected 0 file(s) (0 bytes)     Total 33 file(s) (326KB)
```

Your system will display different directories than the ones shown here, as it is bound to be structured differently. Nonetheless the 'root' directory, indicated by the back-slash sign (\), of a particular drive, is the main directory under which several directories can be found.

In turn, each directory can have its own subdirectories, thus allowing you to keep data of similar applications, such as word processor documents or spreadsheet work-files, together in their respective subdirectories.

The Directory Tree

From the directory tree you can list files within individual directories, or change the logged disc drive. Directories which are marked with a plus sign (+), contain subdirectories. Whether subdirectories appear collapsed and their presence is indicated with a plus sign (+), depends on the selections made within the **Tree** options from the File Manager's menu bar. Double-clicking on such a collapsed icon, opens it up to reveal the subdirectories under it. Such subdirectories are shown below for the case of the WINDOWS directory.

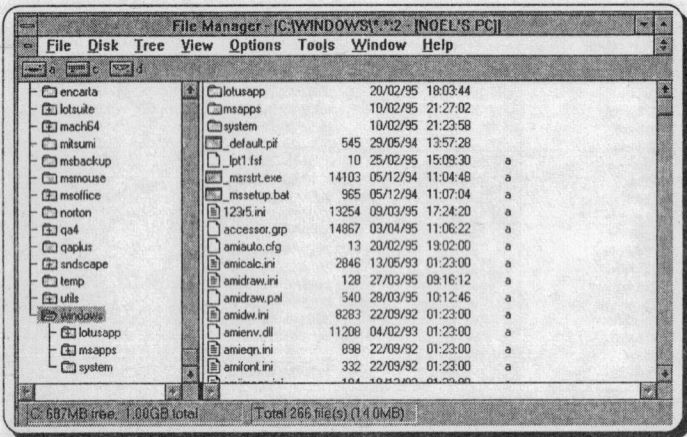

When subdirectories are displayed, the icon of the parent directory appears like an open file (as the one above) and, depending on the selections made within the **Tree** sub-menu, might also acquire a minus sign (–), indicating that it can be collapsed.

The right-hand side of the display is automatically displayed when you select a given directory from the directory tree. The title bar of this window is C:\WINDOWS*.*, indicating that all the files, including subdirectories, are listed.

You can change the information shown in a directory window by using the **View** commands from the File Manager's menu bar.

For example, you could display information on the size of files and the date and time such files were created or last changed, by selecting the **All File Details** option of the **View** command. Such information can be used to find the latest version of a file amongst files with similar names. Note, however, that in the case of directories the size column is not displayed.

The File Manager Commands

The File Command:

The first of six commands (not counting **Help**) on the File Manager's menu bar, is **File**. Clicking on this command (or pressing Alt+F) displays its sub-menu:

File	
Open	Enter
Move...	F7
Copy...	F8
Delete...	Del
Undelete...	
Rename...	
Properties...	Alt+Enter
Run...	
Print...	
Associate...	
Create Directory...	
Search...	
Select Files...	
Exit	

To illustrate how these commands can be used, first create a temporary directory, then search the hard disc for certain files, select some of these and copy them to the temporary directory. We will eventually discuss ways of deleting these files from the temporary directory, including the removal of the created directory itself. So, don't worry, the contents of your hard disc will not be changed.

To create a new directory, select **Create Directory** from the sub-menu of **File** and type a name for it, say **filebin1**, in the **Name** field of the displayed Create Directory dialogue box. On pressing the **OK** button the directory is created and is displayed in the correct alphabetical sequence in the directory tree.

To search a directory, say WINDOWS, for specific files, say those with the **.exe** extension, highlight the WINDOWS directory on the directory tree, then select the **Search** option from the **File** sub-menu and type the information you want to search for, in this case *.exe, as shown below.

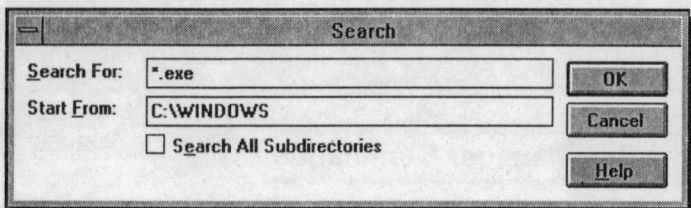

Make sure to remove the cross from the **Search All Subdirectories** box, before pressing the **OK** button, otherwise File Manager will find all the executable files on your hard disc, which can be rather a lot.

The names of the files found are then displayed in a 'Search Results' window as follows:

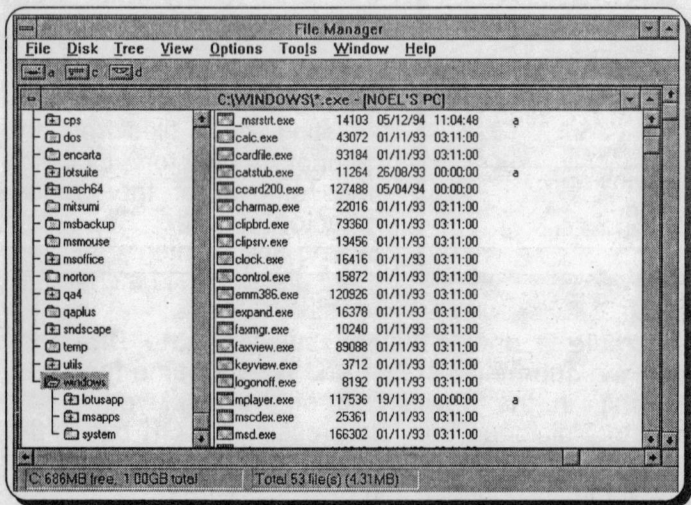

To select a single file to copy, point to it with the mouse and click once to highlight it. If you want to copy a group of contiguous files, then press the <Shift> key and while keeping it pressed select the files at the start and end of the block which results in all files in between being selected. If you want to copy two separate blocks of files, press both the <Ctrl> and the <Shift> key at the same time and while keeping them pressed, select the files at the start and end of the first block, then release the <Shift> key (but keep the <Ctrl> key pressed) and select the first file of the second block, after which, press again the <Shift> key and select the last file of the second block.

To copy all the files in the 'Search Results' window to the **filebin1** directory, choose the **Select Files** option from the **File** sub-menu, accept the default *.* by pressing the **Select** button of the revealed dialogue box, shown here. Once this button has been pressed, the **Cancel** button changes to a **Close** button which you press. Next, choose the **File, Copy** command and type the destination directory, in this case C:**filebin1** (it could be another disc) in the displayed 'Copy To' dialogue box before pressing the **OK** button.

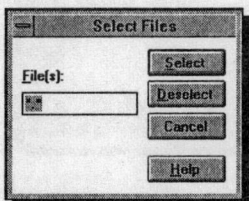

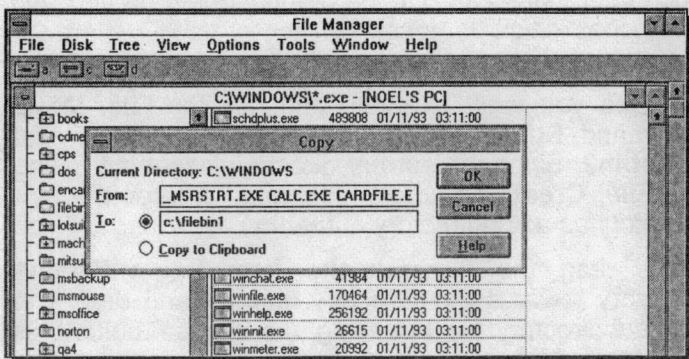

When all the files have been copied, return to the directory tree window and click on the **filebin1** directory icon.

The copied files are now displayed in a separate window with the title **'c:\filebin1*.*'**, as shown below:

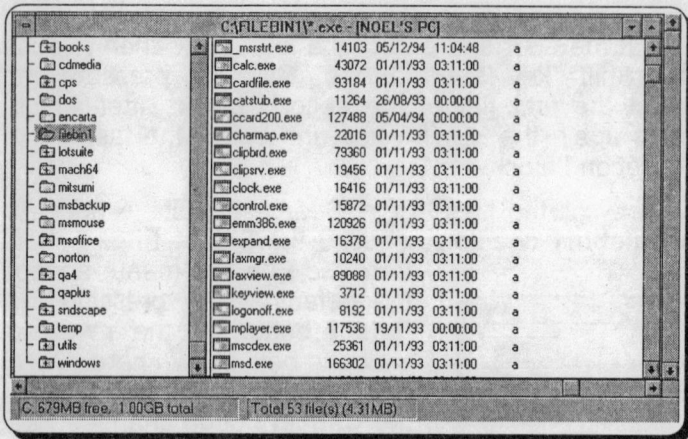

Before you go on, make sure you have created the **filebin1** directory and have copied into it the suggested files. What we are about to demonstrate is how to **move** files from one directory to another, and eventually, how to delete groups of files. Obviously such operations can only be demonstrated on files and directories which do not matter.

To move files from one directory into another, you mark the files you want to move and use the **File, Move** command. But first, let us create another directory - call it **filebin2**. Since the current directory is **filebin1**, using the **File, Create Directory** command creates the new directory as a subdirectory of **filebin1**.

Next, drag the file **calc.exe** from the **c:\filebin1** directory towards the directory **filebin2** and drop it in the subdirectory by releasing the mouse button, as shown overleaf.

Ami Pro - [1STEP05.SAM]

File **Edit** **View** **Text** **Style** **Page** **Frame** **Tools** **Window** **Help**

File Manager

File **Disk** **Tree** **View** **Options** **Tools** **Window** **Help**

C:\FILEBIN1*.exe - [NOEL'S PC]

books	msrstrt.exe	14103	05/12/94 11:04:48	a
cdmedia	calc.exe	43072	01/11/93 03:11:00	a
cps	cardfile.exe	93184	01/11/93 03:11:00	a
dos	catstub.exe	11264	26/08/93 00:00:00	a
encarta	ccard200.exe	127488	05/04/94 00:00:00	a
filebin1	charmap.exe	22016	01/11/93 03:11:00	a
filebin2	clipbrd.exe	79360	01/11/93 03:11:00	a
lotsuite	clipsrv.exe	19456	01/11/93 03:11:00	a
mach64	clock.exe	16416	01/11/93 03:11:00	a
mitsumi	control.exe	15872	01/11/93 03:11:00	a
msbackup	emm386.exe	120926	01/11/93 03:11:00	a
msmouse	expand.exe	16378	01/11/93 03:11:00	a
msoffice	faxmgr.exe	10240	01/11/93 03:11:00	a
norton	faxview.exe	89088	01/11/93 03:11:00	a
qa4	keyview.exe	3712	01/11/93 03:11:00	a
qaplus	logonoff.exe	8192	01/11/93 03:11:00	a
sndscape	mplayer.exe	117536	19/11/93 00:00:00	a
temp	mscdex.exe	25361	01/11/93 03:11:00	a
utils	msd.exe	166302	01/11/93 03:11:00	a

Copying files to C:\FILEBIN1\FILEBIN2

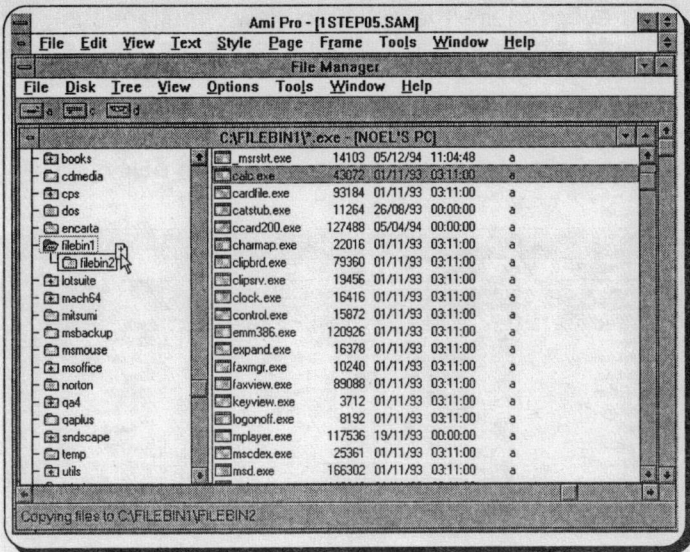

You can now safely delete a directory and its contents by first highlighting its name, and then using the **File**, **Delete** command. You will be asked for confirmation in a Delete dialogue box. Try deleting the **filebin2** subdirectory.

You can rename a directory, even though it contains files, by selecting the **File, Rename** command. Try renaming **filebin1** to **filebin**. Finally, to delete **filebin** and all its contents without having to confirm each file in turn, if you are running Windows 3.1 remove the cross from the **Confirm On File Delete** option in the Confirmation dialogue box of the **Options, Confirmation** command, or if you are running Windows 3.11 press the **Yes to All** button in the Confirm Directory Delete dialogue box.

This, however, is as dangerous as the DOS command **del *.***, so be *very* careful when using it on original files and directories. You will be asked only once if you mean what you say!

If you ever require the ability to view simultaneously the contents of two different directories or disc drives, simply double-click the drive icon to open an additional window for that drive, then select the **Window, Tile** command from the File Manager's menu bar to display both screens at the same time, as shown below.

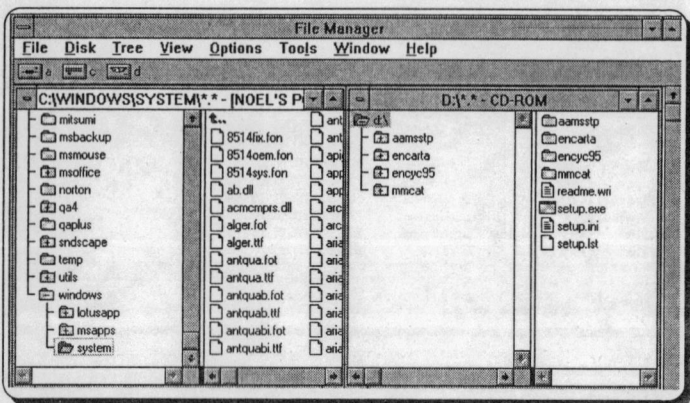

The Disc Command:

The second command on the File Manager's menu bar allows you to perform several different types of operations on floppy discs, as shown on the following **Disk** command's sub-menu:

You can Copy a disc on to another, give a disc a 'Label', 'Format' a disc (advisable for only new discs, as it wipes the disc clean of all data), 'Make a System Disc' by copying on to it the system files, so that you can boot (start) your computer from that disc, or 'Select a Drive', including the selection or deselection of a network drive.

The Tree Command:

The third command on the File Manager's menu bar is **Tree**. Its sub-menu is as follows:

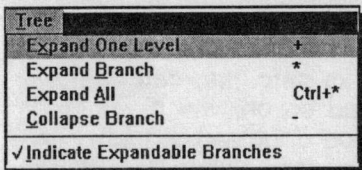

```
Tree
  Expand One Level          +
  Expand Branch             *
  Expand All             Ctrl+*
  Collapse Branch           -
√ Indicate Expandable Branches
```

From here you can control what you see on your directory tree. For example, you can 'Expand a tree one level', 'Expand a branch', 'Expand all' branches, or Collapse a branch'. At the same time, you can 'Indicate expandable branches' with the plus (+) sign and all collapsable branches with the minus (–) sign, by selecting the last option.

The View Command:

The fourth command on the File Manager's menu bar is **View**. Its sub-menu is shown below:

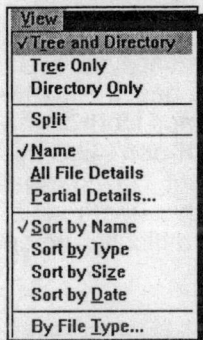

```
View
√ Tree and Directory
  Tree Only
  Directory Only
  Split
√ Name
  All File Details
  Partial Details...
√ Sort by Name
  Sort by Type
  Sort by Size
  Sort by Date
  By File Type...
```

Most of these options are self-explanatory. You can use the **View, All File Details** option to see the file attributes in a directory window. The letters A, H, R, and S are used in the listing against a filename to indicate 'Archive', 'Hidden', 'Read Only', and 'System' files, respectively. Having found out what type of files you are dealing with, you can then change their attributes.

To change such file attributes, first select the file, then use the **File, Properties** command, which causes the 'File Properties' dialogue box to appear on your screen so that you can select or clear the appropriate check boxes.

Most of the other commands in the sub-menus of the File Manager's menu bar, are self-explanatory, therefore we will not pursue this discussion any further.

Starting Applications from File Manager

You can start an application from the File Manager simply by locating its **.exe**, **.com**, **.bat**, or **.pif** file in the application's directory and double-click the filename.

For example, within the WINDOWS directory, you can recognise filenames such as **calc.exe**, **calendar.exe**, **cardfile.exe**, **clock.exe**, and so on, which will start a familiar application when you double-click them. Try it with the **clock.exe**, then look for another file within the WINDOWS directory with the name **msdos.exe**. When you locate it double-click at its name. The program now running is the MS-DOS Executive which is a simpler and earlier version of File Manager. Try exploring the various commands of this program to see how many are similar to those of File Manager. By doing so you will learn a lot about both programs.

Next, change directory to the root directory, double click on the C:\ to reveal the files within the root directory and double-click the **command.com** file. This will open a DOS prompt, either in a window or full screen (depending on your settings) and you must type EXIT to return to the previous application. It has the same effect as double-clicking the DOS Prompt icon of the 'Main' group. Try it as an experiment, but don't use this method to access the DOS prompt in normal circumstances. In one of our PCs this method of accessing the DOS prompt caused difficulty when exiting the DOS window.

6. THE PROGRAM MANAGER

The central and essential element in the Windows operation is Program Manager; it runs whenever you start Windows and continues to do so until you exit Windows. Other programs can be started from within Program Manager simply by double clicking at their icons. While other programs run, Program Manager continues to run in the background or as a minimised icon on your screen, called the 'desktop'.

Program Manager allows you to organise your disc files in logical groups, irrespective of their physical location on the disc. For example, when you first start Windows, Program Manager automatically opens the Main group of applications. Other applications have been gathered together automatically by SETUP and put into the Accessories group, while others have been put into the Games group.

Program Manager not only allows you to regroup applications in your preferred way, but also to make up new application groups with the added convenience of allowing you to include the same application in more than one program group. As an illustration, let us create a new program group, called Utilities, in which we will gather all the useful programs we might need to help us make our system more efficient.

Creating a New Program Group

To create a new program group, use the Program Manager's **File, New** command which displays the dialogue box shown here.

To create a new group, rather than add an item to an existing group, click at the Program **Group** option of the New Program Object dialogue box and press the **OK** button.

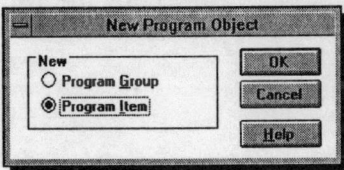

55

This causes the Program Group Properties dialogue box to be displayed, as shown below:

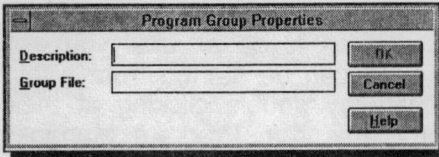

Enter the name 'Utilities' in the **Description** box which will be the name displayed in the title bar of the new group. Pressing <Enter>, will display a new window bearing the name 'Utilities'.

Leave the **Group File** field empty (even though you have the option to type in a different name for the group), because Windows normally assigns it the name you typed in the **Description** box with the extension .GRP in order to be able to find later what programs you have assigned to this group.

To copy a program to the Utilities group window, you must first open the group window where the program you want to copy resides; in our example, the Accessories group. Do this and size both group windows so they are visible on you screen.

A Program application can be copied with the mouse by pressing the <Ctrl> key and while keeping it pressed, dragging the application icon to the desired position within the Utilities window. Releasing the mouse button (and the <Ctrl> key) places a copy of the desired program in the new group window. With the keyboard, use the **File, Copy** command.

If you have copied an application you did not mean to copy, then erase it from its new position by first highlighting it, and then either pressing the <Del> key, or using the **File, Delete** command. Now copy the two applications 'Write' and 'Notepad' to the Utilities window, as shown on the next page.

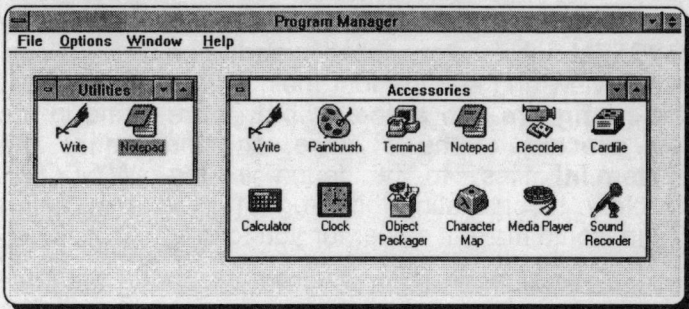

A program application can be moved from one group to another, by either dragging its icon to the new group window or using the **File, Move** command. Try moving the Clock from the Accessories to the Utilities and back again, then copy it to the Utilities.

It is perhaps worth emphasising that by copying or moving an application to another group of programs, you are not producing more copies of the program on your disc or changing the place where your program resides on your disc. You are simply regrouping access to programs is a logical rather than physical way.

Adding Files to a Program Group:

Sometimes you might find it useful to locate a program file that resides on your disc, but is not contained in any of the program groups available to you under the Program Manager, and add it to one of them. Such a program file could be one that you have inadvertently deleted from a program group, or one that was never there in the first place.

To accomplish our task we need to use the File Manager from the Main group of applications to locate such a program file, and drag it to a group within the Program Manager. The File Manager, as we have seen, is a powerful tool that can help with the organisation of files and directories on your disc.

There is a program available within the Windows' \SYSTEM subdirectory called **sysedit.exe** which allows you to view and edit the four main system files, namely the **config.sys** and **autoexec.bat,** to be found in the root directory of the C: drive, and the **win.ini** and **system.ini** files, to be found in the \WINDOWS directory. Incorporating this program within the Utilities group, could make it easier for you to use it.

First, close all application windows except for the Main and Utilities groups (closed applications appear as small icons at the bottom of the Program Manager window). Next, drag the right edge of the Program Manager window to near the middle of your display, then point and double click on the File Manager icon and size its window so it fits in the right half of your display. Now, point and click on the \WINDOWS directory, then click on the SYSTEM subdirectory and scroll to the right until you locate the **sysedit.exe** file and drag its icon into the Utilities group window, as shown below:

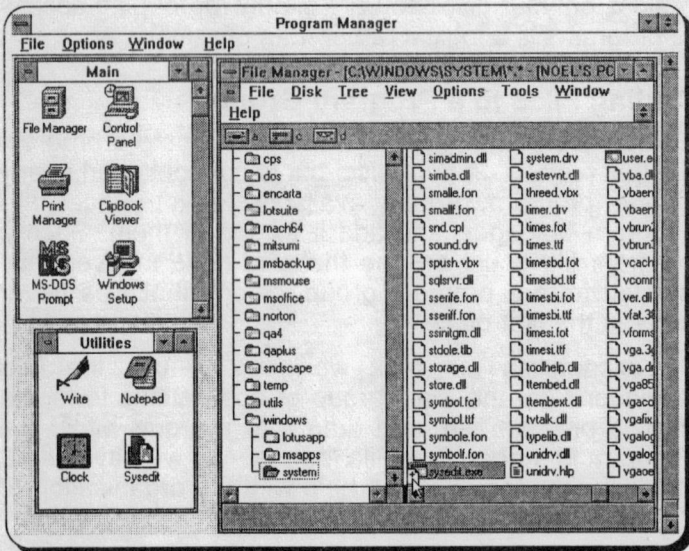

Changing a Group's Properties

To change the description of an individual item within a group, select the icon of the item and use the **File, Properties** command, while to change the description of a whole group of programs, first minimise the group, then select the group icon and use the **File, Properties** command. Limit such descriptions to less than 15 characters long, otherwise they will overlap, unless you use the Control Panel's Desktop module to increase the Icon Spacing, although this changes the spacing for *all* icon labels which decreases the number you can display at once.

With Windows 3.1 and 3.11, you can force a title to appear on two lines provided its name is made up of two words and the total length (including the space between the words) is 13 or more characters long in Windows 3.1 (14 or more in Windows 3.11). To illustrate the point, highlight the File Manager icon within the Main group, then select the **File, Properties** option from the Program Manager's menu which displays the following dialogue box:

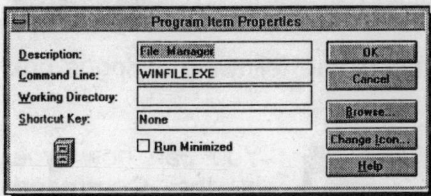

To see the title wrap to a second line, add a space (two spaces in Windows 3.11) between the two words describing the item, so that its length is now equal to the required character limit. On pressing the **OK** button, the description of this item now appears on two lines.

To delete an individual item from within a group, select the item icon and use the **File, Delete** command while to delete a whole group of programs, first minimise the group, then select the group icon and use the **File, Delete** command. In both cases you will be warned with an 'Are you sure' dialogue box before execution.

Adding Windows Applications

Most computers these days are sold pre-loaded with Windows software. However, there will come the time when you will want to buy a special Windows application and this section of the book tells you how to load such an application on to your hard disc.

To load a new Windows application, start Windows, then use the Program Manager's **File, Run** command, as shown below.

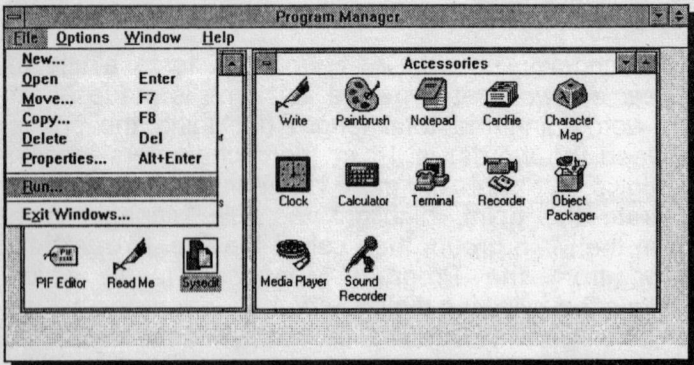

On selecting the command, the following dialogue box opens:

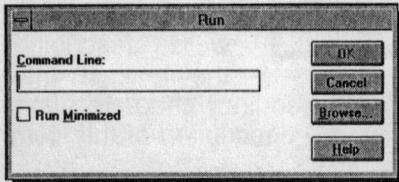

You can now type in the **Command Line** box the name of the application file and the full path, if necessary.

For example, if the application was distributed on diskettes, insert disc #1 into the A: drive and type

```
a:install
```

Some programs require you to type

```
a:setup
```

instead. Usually the name of the installation program is written on disc #1.

If you are not sure of the name of the installation file, you can type A: then press the **Browse** button on the Run dialogue box, which opens an additional dialogue box in which the autoexecution files are listed, as shown below.

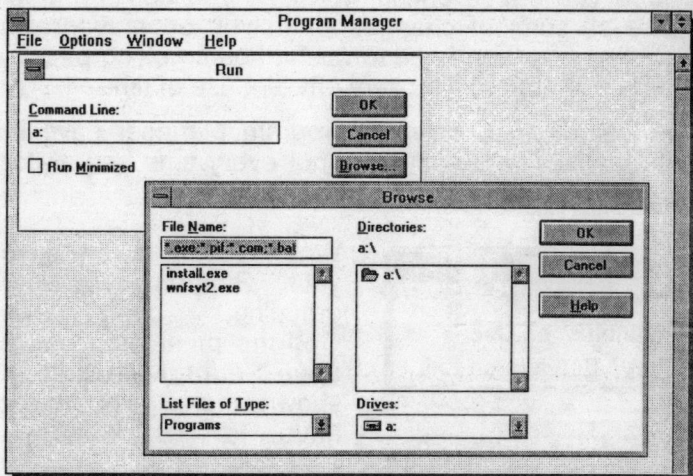

Usually, the file you are looking for has the extension EXE.

Having located the filename of the installation program, select it by clicking on its name, which causes it to be transferred to the Run dialogue box. Pressing the **OK** button, starts the installation of your software. When a new disc is required, the installation program will inform you. When all discs have been read, the installation program will create and display a new group of icons and will modify your system files automatically so that you can start the application easily.

Saving Program Manager Settings

When you first start using Windows, one of the hardest things to come to terms with is that the screen layout you spent so long on, no longer seems to be there the next time you open Windows. Some self-discipline is required, whenever you set up or make changes to your layout.

Once you are happy with your Program Manager grouping, make sure you save and then protect it, before you start working with it. If you don't, you will make all sorts of changes when you open programs and files and then have to spend hours getting back to where you started. Not very efficient use of time.

The secret is to only let Program Manager save its set-up when you want it to, not every time you switch off, which is the default.

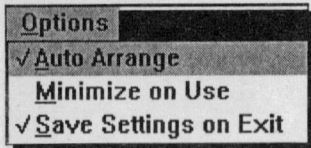

When you want to save your Program Manager grouping, open the **Options** menu and select **Save Settings on Exit** as shown here. You don't have to exit Windows though to activate this, as you can use the <Shift+Alt+F4> key combination to save the settings only. An alternative way of doing this is to open the **File** menu, and with the <Shift> key held down select **Exit Windows** from the drop-down menu.

The important step now is to switch off settings saving by again selecting **Save Settings on Exit** from the **Options** menu. This will remove the tick symbol (√) from the menu listing.

Now whatever mess your screen is in when you close down Windows, it should be all neat and tidy for your next session. Don't forget though, continuous self-discipline here is important!

7. THE PRINT MANAGER

You can use Print Manager to print information from a Windows application. Obviously, there might be some differences from one application to another, but these are slight.

When you print from a Windows application, the application creates a print file which is sent to the Windows Print Manager. From then on, Print Manager looks after the printing, queueing print files as they are sent to it, and freeing the application so that you can carry on working while files are being printed. It is assumed, of course, that you have installed your printer and configured it, using the Control Panel.

If you have not, then double-click at the Control Panel icon of the Main group, shown here, and then double-click at the Printers icon in the Control Panel window, shown below.

When you print from a non-Windows application that you have started from within Windows, the application does not use Print Manager - it prints just as it would if you had started it direct from the DOS Prompt.

Checking the Windows Printer Set-up:

When Windows was first installed on your computer the printers you intend to use with your Windows applications should have been selected, and the SETUP program should have installed the appropriate printer drivers. Before printing for the first time with any application, you would be wise to ensure that your printer is in fact properly installed. To do this, double-click on the 'Printers' icon in the Windows Control Panel, shown here, which causes the following Printers dialogue box to be opened.

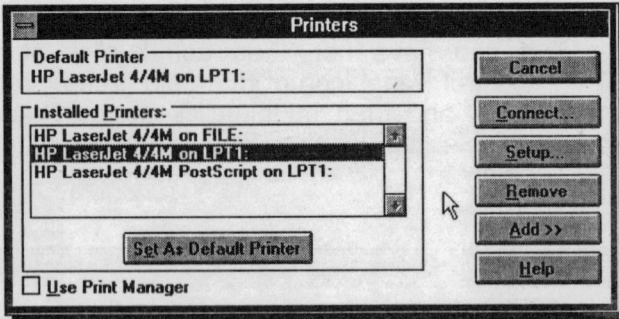

Here, two printer drivers have been installed. An HP LaserJet 4/4M as the 'default' (the printer's name is highlighted and it also appears in the Default Printer box), configured to print to the parallel printer port LPT1, and an HP LaserJet 4/4M PostScript, also configured to print to the parallel printer port. The first printer has also been configured for output to a disc file. Obviously, your selections will not be the same.

Any of the other installed printers can be made the default by highlighting their name and pressing the **Set As Default Printer** button. The **Setup** button allows you to select the size of paper and orientation of printout (portrait or landscape).

Best printed output results are obtained when using a laser printer. So, if you want to produce high quality documents, and you have access to a laser printer (even if it is not connected to your computer and does not itself have access to the particular application you are using), then install the laser printer as an additional printer to be used with Windows and configure it to print to 'File'. To do this, first select the printer in the 'Printers' dialogue box, click the **Connect** button to open the dialogue box displayed below and select **File:** from the list of available printer **Ports**.

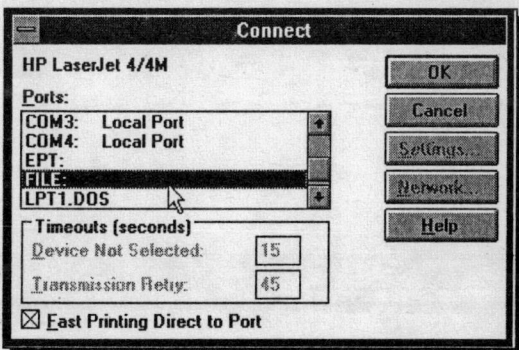

In the future when you select this printer, your work will be printed to a file on disc and you can then copy that file to the laser printer from its attached PC by issuing the simple DOS command

```
COPY Filename LPT1: /B
```

The /B switch in this command tells the printer to expect a binary file; without this the process may, or may not work. So it is safer to use it.

To install a different printer, press the **Add** button in the 'Printers' dialogue box, choose a printer from the list displayed, and select **Install**. Each time you choose to install a different printer, Windows will ask you to insert a particular Windows disc in drive A:, so that the appropriate driver can be copied on to your hard disc.

The Print Queue

When you print to a local printer, Print Manager maintains a local print queue which is a list of files that have been sent from an application to the printer. When Print Manager starts printing to a local queue, its icon appears at the bottom of your screen and enlarging it allows you to see the print queue, as follows:

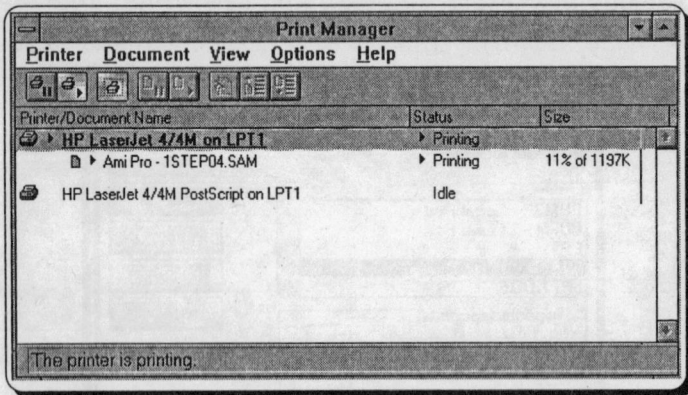

The above screen was obtained by using the <Alt+Tab> key combination to go to the Print Manager, after starting a print command from within a word processor. Had you double-clicked the Print Manager icon, shown here (to be found in Program Manager's Main group), you would have obtained the same screen as the one above, but the status of both printers would have been idle.

Having activated the Print Manager dialogue box while printing, you could change the order of printing of files to a local printer by simply selecting the name of the file you want to move and dragging it to the required position in the queue.

When Print Manager prints to a network queue, the file is sent directly to the network print server. To see the state of the queue, you must double-click at the Print Manager icon of the Main group of applications - there is no Print Manager icon at the bottom of your screen as there is when printing locally. However, you cannot change the order of files in a network queue.

Finally, you can delete a file from a print queue, by selecting the file and pressing the **Delete** button on the Print Manager window, or you can delete all files in the queue by choosing the **Options, Exit** command, and pressing the **OK** button of the displayed confirmation dialogue box.

Printing to a Switchable or Network Printer

Normally, when printing under Windows, documents are sent directly to the printer connected to your system, bypassing the MS-DOS printing interrupts, which speeds up printing.

However, if you are trying to print to a switchable or a network printer which has been assigned to, say, the parallel port LPT1, then you must specify the location of the printer and use the MS-DOS interrupts. To do this, select the **Printer Setup** option from the Print Manager's **Options** menu, as shown below.

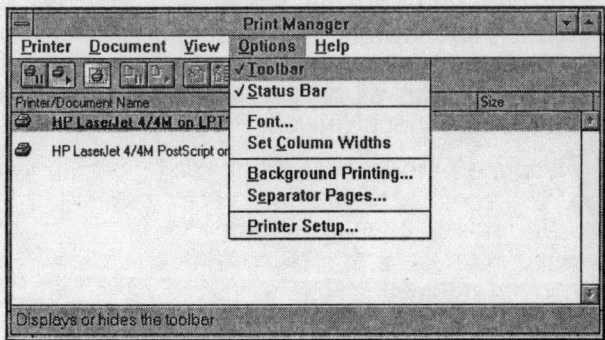

This opens the Printers dialogue box, and pressing the **Connect** button reveals the Connect dialogue box, as shown below.

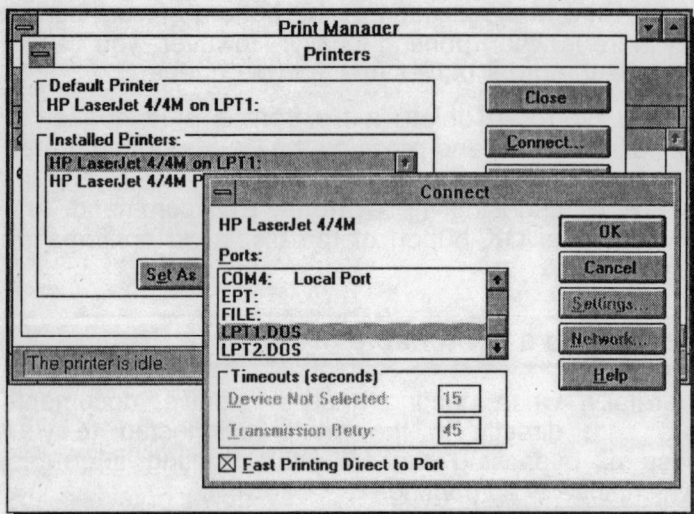

If you are printing to a switchable printer which is controlled by software, clear the **Fast Printing Direct to Port** check box and press the **OK** button.

If you are printing to a network printer, in addition to clearing the above check box, also scroll down the list of **Ports** until you find the printer port that has been assigned to your network printer, say, LPT1.DOS. Next, press the **Network** button (if you are connected to a network this facility will be available to you), and fill in the displayed Connect Network Printer dialogue box.

8. GLOSSARY OF TERMS

Active	The window or icon that is currently selected or you are currently using.
ANSI	A complete 256 character set used by Windows. The first 128 characters are the same as the ASCII standard used by DOS applications.
Application	Software (program) designed to carry out certain activity, such as word processing.
Application icon	An icon that represents a running application. The icon only appears after you minimise an application.
Application window	The window containing the work area and menu bar for an application. An application may contain multiple document windows.
Arrow keys	The keys on the keyboard that you use to navigate around the screen.
ASCII	See ANSI.
Autoexec.bat	A batch file containing commands which are automatically executed on start-up.
Background application	An application that is running but is not active.
Base memory	The first 1 Mbyte of RAM.
Batch file	An ASCII formatted file that contains executable DOS commands.

Binary file	A file with machine-readable information; it can be read only by an application.
Bit	A binary digit; the smallest unit of information that can be stored, either as 1 or 0.
Bitmap	A technique for managing the image displayed on a computer screen.
Browse	To look through files and directories. A Browse button in a dialogue box, lists files and directories for you to select.
Byte	A group of binary digits (0 or 1) representing information.
Cache	An area of memory reserved for data, which speeds up access to a disc.
Click	To quickly press and release a mouse button.
Clipboard	An area of memory (also called a buffer), where text, graphics, and commands can be stored to await further action.
Command	An instruction given to a PC.
Command.com	The Operating System's Command Processor. It analyses typed information and executes appropriate commands.
Command line	The line on the computer's screen into which you enter DOS commands.

Command Prompt	See System Prompt.
Config.sys	A special file that allows the system to be configured closer to requirement.
Control menu	A menu that contains commands you can use to manipulate a window.
Conventional Memory	The first 640 KB of base memory, used by DOS programs.
Current directory	The directory that is searched first for a requested file.
Data file	A file created within an application, such as a word processing document.
Default	The command, device or option automatically chosen by the system.
Desktop	The screen background for Windows on which windows, icons, and dialogue boxes appear.
Device driver	A set of commands used to run a peripheral device.
Device name	A logical name used by DOS to identify a device, such as LPT1 or COM1 for the parallel or serial printer.
Dialogue box	A box that displays on the screen for the user to supply more information.
Directory	An area on disc where information relating to a group of files is kept.

Directory tree	A pictorial representation of your disc's structure.
Disc	A device on which you can store programs and data.
Disc cache	A portion of memory set aside for temporarily holding information read from a disc.
Disc file	A collection of program code, or data, that is stored under a given name on a disc.
Display adapter	A hardware device that converts video memory to video output.
Document	Work created with an application.
Document window	A window within an application window.
DOS	The Disc Operating System. A collection of small specialised programs that allow you to interact with your PC.
DOS prompt	See System Prompt.
Double-click	To quickly press and release a mouse button twice.
DPI	Dots Per Inch - a resolution standard for laser printers.
Drag	To press and hold down the left mouse button while moving the mouse.
Drive name	The letter followed by a colon which identifies a floppy or hard disc drive.

Driver	See Device driver.
Enter key	The key that must be pressed after entering data.
Extended memory	This is memory above the 1-Mbyte memory address which DOS can use for certain operations.
Extension	The period and up to three characters at the end of a filename.
File	An area on disc containing a program or data.
File extension	See Extension.
File list	A list of filenames contained in the active directory.
Filename	The name given to a file. It must not exceed 8 characters in length and can have an extension of up to 3 characters.
Filespec	File specification made up of drive, path, filename and a three letter extension.
Fixed disc	See Hard disc.
Foreground	The area on the screen that the active window occupies.
Floppy disc	A removable 5¼" or 3½" disc.
Function key	One of the series of 10 or 12 keys marked with the letter F and a numeral, used for specific operations.
Gigabyte	1,024 Megabytes.

Graphics card	A device that controls the display on the monitor and other allied functions.
Group	A collection of applications, accessories or documents within Program Manager.
GUI	A Graphical User Interface used by Windows and Windows applications that uses graphics to eliminate the need for typing commands.
Hard disc	A device built into the PC for holding programs and data.
Hardware	The equipment that makes up a computer system, but not programs or software.
Help	A feature that gives you instructions and additional information.
Hidden files	Files that do not normally appear in a directory listing.
Highlight	The change to a reverse-video appearance when a menu item or area of text is selected.
Icon	A small graphic image that represents a function. Clicking on an icon produces an action.
Inactive window	Any open window that you are not currently working in.
Initialisation file	A file with the extension .INI that holds information relating to your Windows environment.

Interface	A device that allows you to connect a computer to its peripherals.
Kilobyte	(KB); 1024 bytes of information or storage space.
LAN	Local Area Network; computers sharing files and peripherals within a site.
List box	A box in a Windows application or dialogue box that lists available choices.
Local printer	A printer that is directly connected to one of the ports on your computer.
LPT port	See Parallel port.
Megabyte	(MB); 1024 kilobytes of information or storage space.
Megahertz	(MHz); Speed of processor in million of cycles per second.
Memory	Storage elements organised into addressable locations that can hold data and instructions.
Menu	A list of available options as appears in Windows.
Menu bar	The horizontal bar that lists the names of menus.
Microprocessor	The calculating chip within a computer.
Monitor	The display device connected to your computer.
Mouse	A pointing device used to move around a display and

	activate a certain process by pressing a button.
MS-DOS	Microsoft's implementation of DOS for compatible PCs.
Multimedia	A combination of various media, such as graphics, sound, and video.
Multitasking	A computer's ability to run more than one application at the same time.
Network printer	A printer shared by computers connected to a network.
Network server	Central computer which stores files for several linked computers.
Operating System	See DOS.
Parallel interface	A device that allows transfer of blocks of data in bytes.
Parallel port	A connection on a PC, usually LPT1, where you plug the cable for a parallel printer.
PATH	The drive and directories that DOS should look in for files.
PC	Personal Computer.
PCX	A standard file format used for bitmapped graphics.
Peripheral	Any device attached to a computer.
PIF	Program information file - it provides information about how Windows should run a non-Windows application.

Pixel	A picture element on screen; the smallest element that can be assigned colour and intensity.
Port	An input/output address through which your PC interacts with external devices.
Printer driver	A program that controls how your computer and printer interact.
Print queue	The list of print jobs waiting to be sent to a printer.
Program	A set of instructions which cause the computer to perform certain tasks.
Program file	An executable file that starts an application or program - it has an .exe, .com, .pif, or .bat extension.
Prompt	See System Prompt.
Protected mode	The operating mode of 286 (and higher) processors, not normally used by DOS. It allows more than 1 Mbyte of memory to be addressed.
Processor	The electronic device which performs calculations.
RAM	Random Access Memory. The micro's volatile memory. Data held in it is lost when power is switched off.
Real mode	The normal operating mode of PCs, in which only the first 1 Mbyte of memory can be addressed.

ROM	Read Only Memory. The micro's non-volatile memory. Data are written into it at manufacture and are not affected by power loss.
Root directory	The main disc directory under which a number of sub-directories can be created.
Screen saver	A moving picture or pattern that appears on your screen when you have not moved the mouse or pressed a key in Windows for a specified period of time.
Sector	Disc space, normally 512 bytes long.
Serial interface	An interface that transfers data as individual bits; each operation is completed before the next starts.
Serial printer	A printer using a serial interface, which you connect to the serial port.
Serial port	A connection on a computer, usually COM1, where you plug in the cable for a serial device, such as a printer or a modem.
Software	The programs and instructions that control your PC's functionality.
Standard mode	A Windows operating mode that can be used with 80286 and higher processors.
Subdirectory	A directory within another directory.

SVGA	Super Video Graphics Array; it has all the VGA modes but with 256 colours.
Swap file	An area of the hard disc that is set aside for exclusive use by Windows in 386 enhanced mode. It is used to transfer temporarily information from memory to disc to free memory for other use.
System	Short for computer system, implying a specific collection of hardware and software.
System disc	A disc containing DOS' three main files and other Utilities.
System prompt	The prompt displayed on the screen, such as A> or C> indicating that DOS is ready to accept commands.
Task List	A window that shows all applications you are running and enables you to switch between them.
Text editor	An application, such as Notepad, used to create, view, and modify text files.
Text file	A file saved in ASCII format. It contains text characters, but no formatting codes.
TSR	Terminate and Stay Resident programs, that is, memory resident programs.
Upper memory	The 384 Kbytes of memory between the top of

	conventional memory and the end of the base memory.
VGA	Video Graphics Array; has all modes of EGA, but with 16 colours.
Virtual memory	A memory management system used by Windows in 386 enhanced mode that enables Windows to run as if there were more memory than is actually present.
Volume label	An identifying label written to a disc.
Wallpaper	An image being displayed on Windows' desktop.
Wildcard character	A character that can be included in a filename to indicate any character (?) or group of characters (*) that might match that position in other filenames.
WIN.INI	A Windows initialisation file that contains settings you can use to customise your Windows environment.
Window	An area on your screen in which you can view an application or document.
Windows	A program developed by Microsoft in which applications can appear in graphical form.
Windows application	An application that is designed to run under Windows.

INDEX

COMPANION DISC TO THIS BOOK

This book contains several example file listings. There is no reason why you should type them yourself into your computer, unless you wish to do so, or need the practice.

The COMPANION DISC comes with all these listings, ready for you to load them into the program described in the book.

COMPANION DISCS for most books written by the same author(s) are also available and are listed (without an asterisk) at the front of this book. **Make sure you fill in your name and address** and specify the book number and title in your order.

ORDERING INSTRUCTIONS
To obtain your copy of the companion disc, fill in the order form below, or a copy of it, enclose a cheque (payable to **P.R.M. Oliver**) or a postal order, and send it to the address given below.

Book No.	Book Name	Unit Price	Total Price
BP		£3.50	
BP		£3.50	
BP		£3.50	
Name		Sub-total	£.............
Address		P & P (@ 45p/disc)	£.............
		Total Due	£.............

Send to: P.R.M. Oliver, CSM, Pool, Redruth, Cornwall, TR15 3SE